Self-guided

Salzburg &
The Sound of Music

Written and researched by Brett Harriman

2015

©Map hand-drawn by Brett Harriman

Self-guided

Salzburg &
The Sound of Music

Contents

This guidebook is updated every year. It is the very latest resource on Salzburg, the lake district, and DIY Sound of Music to hit the market. (In essence, there is no single regularly printed guidebook regarding these sites and attractions that is more current and comprehensive than this resource.) While many publishers of guidebooks update their material every so often, "Harriman Travel Books" is as consistent as the resplendent beds of tulips blossoming every spring in the gardens at Schloss Hellbrunn. Although some details will invariably change after the research has been logged, the vast majority of information is accurate and reliable. I personally visit the sites contained within this guidebook every autumn and therefore it is released with the utmost "freshness" for the coming year. Moreover, it is designed for you to travel like a local, to save time and money, to experience an enjoyable and authentic trip, while leading to new adventures and acquaintances along the way. Thank you for your support, and please tell others about "Harriman Travel Books" — Brett Harriman

Please note when using this guidebook, I've written all times using the 24-hour clock. Europeans exclusively use this system to keep time. Here are the conversions:

1:00 = 1 a.m.	13:00 = 1 p.m.
2:00 = 2 a.m.	14:00 = 2 p.m.
3:00 = 3 a.m.	15:00 = 3 p.m.
4:00 = 4 a.m.	16:00 = 4 p.m.
5:00 = 5 a.m.	17:00 = 5 p.m.
6:00 = 6 a.m.	18:00 = 6 p.m.
7:00 = 7 a.m.	19:00 = 7 p.m.
8:00 = 8 a.m.	20:00 = 8 p.m.
9:00 = 9 a.m.	21:00 = 9 p.m.
10:00 = 10 a.m.	22:00 = 10 p.m.
11:00 = 11 a.m.	23:00 = 11 p.m.
12:00 = 12 p.m.	00:00 = midnight

Salzburg Old Town as seen from Kapuzinerberg   ©Brett Harriman

Salzburg

Population: 150,001. **Elevation:** 450 m (1,480 ft).
Country-Area code: +43-(0)662. **License plate:** S.

In 17 A.D. Romans settled "Iuvavum," a majestic outpost on the banks of a jade-green river that bisected the forested Mönchsberg (Monks' Ridge) and Kapuzinerberg (Capuchins' Ridge). It wasn't long before the region's valuable salt deposits were discovered. The Romans used salt as a food preservative and a commodity to barter goods. They even paid their legionnaires with the "white gold"; hence the term we use today, "salary" (from the Latin "salarium," referring to the salt allotment issued to Roman soldiers for money). Iuvavum blossomed and the population swelled to 5,000. By the year 477, the once vast and mighty Roman Empire had collapsed and Iuvavum fell to nomadic tribes.

In 696 A.D., the Catholic Church dispatched Bishop Rupert from the German city of Worms to form a diocese on the ruins of Iuvavum. He founded St. Peter's monastery, bringing peace, prosperity and Christianity to the region. From these pious roots came the first archbishop, Virgil, and the community's new name: Salzburg (meaning Salt Castle, first mentioned in 755). Appropriately, the jade-green river flowing through Salzburg was also given a name: Salzach, or Salt River—not because of any salt content, but for the prosperous river trade that transported the "white gold" downstream to the Inn River, which flowed into the Danube and eventually the Black Sea and into the coffers of powerful Asian rulers. Bishop Rupert's city of salt flourished, and Salzburg over the next 1,000 years became a wealthy archbishopric, an independent church state ruled by the resident

Catholic prince-archbishop, not the Habsburg emperor seated in Vienna. Salzburg is Austria's only city that can claim its own history of autonomy from the imperial family.

In 1803, Napoleon's troops arrived and secularized the millennium-old diocese, forcing the last archbishop (Hieronymus) to flee to Vienna. It wasn't until 1816 that Salzburg actually became part of Austria.

More than a century later, Austria joined forces with Hitler's ill-fated Third Reich, consequently attracting swarms of Allied aircraft to the city of salt. From October 1944 till the end of World War II (May 1945), there were 16 bombing raids over Salzburg, totaling some 750 bombers (mainly B-24s), leaving 46% of the city's buildings either lightly or heavily damaged. Salzburg, however, didn't take long to recover and today the antique settlement on the Salt River has never looked better. What's more, since 1996, Salzburg's Altstadt has taken its place alongside the historic old towns of Brugge (Belgium), Dubrovnik (Croatia), and Florence (Italy) as an esteemed member of UNESCO's World Heritage List. For this reason, Salzburg's Old Town has largely been pedestrianized and its buses are smog-free, powered by electricity (overhead electrical lines).

According to a reliable source, 1 in 5 Salzburgers work in the service and tourism industry, and the city's single biggest private employer outside of this broad field is the Stiegl Brewing company with more than 650 employees. But tourism remains the city's No. 1 money-spinner, attracting nearly 7 million visitors per year. Next to the federal capital of Vienna, Salzburg is Austria's second most important tourist destination. I, your humble author, have personally escorted some 6,000 guests through Salzburg, and not one was ever disappointed! Now it is *your* turn to marvel the majesty that is this magnificent municipality.

SALZBURG	Average Rainfall	Sun Hours	Average Temps	Highest / Lowest Temps
January	60 mm (2.36 in)	67	-1°C (30F)	16°C (61F) /-25.5°C (-14F)
February	55 mm (2.16 in)	91.9	1°C (34F)	22°C (72F) / -22°C (-7.5F)
March	79 mm (3.11 in)	130	5°C (41F)	25°C (77F) / -21.5°C (-7F)
April	83 mm (3.26 in)	152.6	8.5°C (47F)	28°C (82F) / -4°C (25F)
May	114.5 mm (4.5 in)	196.4	14°C (57F)	32°C (90F) / -2°C (28F)
June	155 mm (6.1 in)	193.9	17°C (63F)	35.5°C (96F) / 2°C (35.5F)
July	157.5 mm (6.2 in)	221.1	19°C (66F)	38°C (100F) / 4°C (39F)
August	151 mm (5.94 in)	202.8	18°C (64F)	35.5°C (96F) / 4°C (39F)
September	101 mm (3.97 in)	167.7	14°C (57F)	32°C (90F) / -1.5°C (29F)
October	72.5 mm (2.85 in)	129.7	9°C (48F)	28°C (82F) / -8°C (17.5F)
November	83 mm (3.26 in)	81.2	3.5°C (38F)	23.5°C (74F) / -18°C (-1F)
December	73 mm (2.87 in)	62.8	0.5°C (33F)	18.5°C (65F) /-27°C (-17F)

Climate, Salzburg:

(Salzburg Tourism kindly imparted the following text:) "The city of Salzburg is located next to the Prealps and therefore is very much influenced by the Alpine climate. Winters are usually quite cold and dry; snow can be found pretty often. Summers are hot and friendly, however, rainy periods occur and can last for a couple of days in the 'worst case.' Like with any trip, bringing an umbrella and rain jacket is no mistake — just in case you get acquainted with the famous 'Schnürlregen.'"

In the table above I've entered the results of a 30-year climate study (1971-2000) completed by the Austrian Institute of Meteorology (www.zamg.ac.at). The first three columns average the monthly (air) temperatures, rainfall and amount of sunshine hours in Salzburg over the three-decade period. The fourth column lists the air-temperature highs and lows for that particular month dating from 1971.

Suggested Itinerary: Use Salzburg as your base to tour regional attractions; thus I suggest at least a three-day stay. Mood and weather permitting, divide your time like so:

Day 1: At Mozartplatz set off on my self-guided orientation tour of the city (page 11). Buy the Salzburg Card (page 9) and visit sites of interest. Sound of Music fans, combine the aforesaid city orientation tour with my SOM Walking Tour (page 86). Conclude your day on the Stein Terrasse (page 38) then dinner at the Bärenwirt (page 47), Zum Fideln Affen (page 47), or splurge on the Mozart Dinner Concert (page 43). **Note:** Because public transportation is efficient and 100-percent free with your Salzburg Card, ignore the (overpriced and redundant) yellow Hop On Hop Off sightseer bus regularly circuiting through town. (Locals often refer to it as the Geisterbus, or 'ghost bus,' because outside of the peak summer months it's virtually always empty as it motors past.)

Day 2: Continue touring sites of interest with your Salzburg Card, or travel 25 km southwest to the Bavarian village of Berchtesgaden (see my "Self-guided Berchtesgaden & Hitler's Eagle's Nest" guide) to tour the Eagle's Nest, Königssee lake, and/or salt mines. (Consider purchasing the Bayern-Ticket if traveling by bus, page 6.) For lunch in Berchtesgaden, pack a picnic, or head to the Goldener Bär on the main pedestrian drag, or for more money jump up to the scenic outdoor Panorama restaurant on the rooftop of the newly built Hotel Edelweiss in view of the Berchtesgadener Alps and the Eagle's Nest. Back in Salzburg, consider an evening with the puppets at the Marionette Theater or perhaps take in a classical concert in the fortress or Mirabell Palace (page 43).

Day 3: Consider a trip south to the village of Werfen to experience the lofty ice caves and medieval fortress (page 66) or head east for a day in the Salzkammergut (page 69), conceivably the world's most beautiful lake district.

Children: On vacation with the little ones and wondering what to do in town to pique their interest? See the boxed entry for **Children** on the next page.

👍 **Don't miss it!:** (Note: On my do-it-yourself orientation tour of Salzburg I walk you past, or point out, all of the following listings.) Climb the **Glockenspiel** (page 15); admire the **Cathedral** (page 16); tour the **Fortress** (page 17); stroll through **St. Peter's Cemetery** (page 18) and into **St. Peter's Church** (page 19); stop by **St. Peter's Stiftskeller** (page 46); sample a chocolate **Mozart ball** (page 39); window-shop **Getreidegasse** (page 40); warm up to a shot at **Sporer wines & spirits** (page 40); breath in the exquisiteness of the **Mirabell Gardens** (page 25); take a spell at one of Austria's most scenic café's, the **Stein Terrasse** (page 38); beer drinkers, blow the froth off a couple at **Müllner Bräu** (page 42) or the **Stiegl Keller** (page 46); and lastly, the **Salzburg Card** (page 9) is a must (and since the card is your key to the city, a whole other round of sites and attractions are worth visiting, that is if you have the time, such as: the Untersberg cable car (page 35), Residenz (page 15), Mozart's birthplace (page 22) and Wohnhaus (page 26), boat ride (page 23), Monchberg Lift (page 31), Schloss Hellbrunn and zoo (pages 32-33).

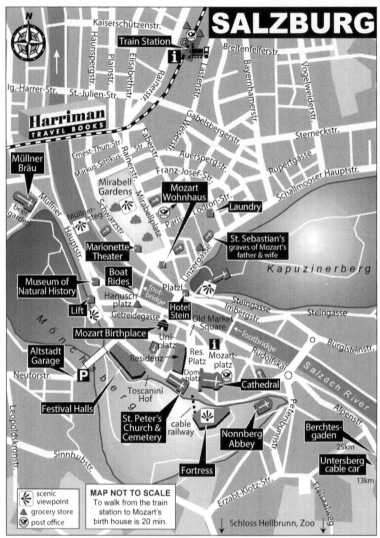

Children: Popular things kids enjoy to do, see or eat in Salzburg are the **Fortress** (pages 17/29); **Glockenspiel tour** (page 15); **Museum of Natural History** (page 31); **Schloss Hellbrunn and zoo** (pages 32-33); DIY **Catacombs tour** (page 30); **Marionette Theater** (page 43); self-guided **Sound of Music tour** (page 82—watch movie first at JUFA hostel-hotel, page 53, combined with cafeteria dinner); **Mozart ball** (page 39); **Mönchsberg Lift & Hiking Trails** (page 38); **Untersberg cable car** (page 35); **Austria's longest toboggan run** (luge ride) combined with neighboring **salt mines** at Dürrnberg (pages 36-37); lunch/dinner at "**Café-Restaurant**" (page 47), **Wilden Mann** (page 46), **Bärenwirt** (page 47), or **Bosna Grill** (page 50).

ORIENTATION

Tourist Information, (www.salzburg.info, tel. 0662/8898-7330, CC: VC, MC, DC). Salzburg has a trio of TIs, offering help and advice to hundreds of tourists every day. To complement this guidebook, stop by the TI and pick up a free city map. Staff also provide a room-finding service for 2.20€, or search free online via the TI website.

Old Town: The largest of the city's three TIs is on Mozartplatz, centrally located in the Old Town (closed Sunday Sept thru March, otherwise daily 9:00-18:00, July/Aug till 19:00). This main branch has an event ticket agency, and offers a (German-English) guided city tour (departing daily at 12:15, duration 60 min, pay guide 9€ adult or 7€ with Salzburg Card, and Mon-Sat at 14:00, duration 60-90 min, 10€/8€); see TI for details.

Railers, most convenient for you is the new TI (daily 9:00-18:00, May/June & Sept 9:00-19:00, July/Aug till 19:30) located inside the main entrance of the train station (on right side in corner hall when entering station). This branch also sells event tickets, e.g. concerts at Mirabell Palace.

Drivers, best suited for you is Süd TI, packed into a portable at the Park+Ride lot off the A10 autobahn. Exit Salzburg-Süd and drive towards Salzburg—after about 4 km follow TI sign to the right. Hours here vary but generally: closed Oct thru Nov 18 as well as Jan thru April, otherwise May & June Thur-Sat 9:00-16:00, July Mon-Sat 9:00-17:00, Aug Mon-Sat 9:00-17:00 & Sun 9:00-16:00, Sept Wed-Sat 9:00-16:00, and Nov 19 thru New Year Thur-Sat 10:00-16:30.

Emergency Tel. Numbers, valid free Austria-wide, dial **122** for the Fire Department (Feuerwehr), **133** for Police (Polizei), or **144** for Ambulance/Rescue.

Main Train Station, (www.oebb.at). This year city officials peeled back the curtain on Salzburg's enlarged Hauptbahnhof (Hbf) concluding its multiyear reconstruction. Thus, as you step off the train and make your way through the station, be sure to compliment its multimillion-euro shine. Pick up a free city map at the **tourist information office** (in corner hall near station's main entrance, daily 9:00-18:00, May/June & Sept 9:00-19:00, July/Aug till 19:30). **Toilets** (.50¢) and **lockers** (2€-4.50€/24hr) are located below track 5, in the main hall. The **ÖBB** (Reisezentrum) **train info** and **ticket purchase** office (Mon-Sat 5:30-21:15, Sun 6:30-21:15) are situated in the main hall straight inside the station's front entrance. Note that also represented in the ÖBB info office is a clerk from the **German rail authority**, Deutsche Bahn (DB), daily 7:00-19:00, imparting state rail info as well as selling tickets for Germany, e.g. the discounted Bayern-Ticket (see next page for details). Directly across from the ÖBB info and ticket office in the main hall is a **Spar grocery store** open seven days (Mon-Sat 6:00-23:00, Sun 8:00-23:00). An **Internet** café is immediately outside the station (exit right, 3€/hr daily 8:00-22:00) or you can pick up **free Wi-Fi** (Mon-Sat till about 19:00) beaming from the "Forum 1" shopping mall outside the station (exit front and angle right; you'll find a McDonald's and Starbucks here). Local **bus connections**, as well as those to Berchtesgaden, are out front of the station. **Taxis** are abundant and also out front. In the "Forum 1" shopping mall outside the station (exit front and angle right) is a **pharmacy** (Apotheke Mon-Fri 8:00-18:00, Sat 8:00-12:00) and a large EuroSpar **supermarket** (all major CCs accepted, Mon-Fri 7:00-19:00, Sat 7:00-18:00). Also outside the station and to the right, past Burger King, is a **post office** (Mon-Fri 8:00-20:30, Sat 8:00-14:00, Sun 13:00-18:00). **Getting to the Old Town** from the station is a painless 20-min *walk, about 8€ by taxi, or ride bus 3, 5 or 6 headed direction Zentrum and get off after a handful of stops at Rathaus. *By foot, exit front of station, go left and continue straight along Rainerstrasse for some distance, eventually leading under the train tracks (this part of the walk is not so nice). A couple of cross streets farther, opposite the church, cut right through the enchanting Mirabell Gardens and traverse the river. **By train from Salzburg to Innsbruck** 2hr trip (roughly every hour 6:00-22:00); **Vienna** 3hr trip (hrly from 5:00 until roughly 22:00); **Melk** 3hr trip (hrly from 5:00 until roughly 22:00, one change); **Berchtesgaden** 85-min trip (hrly with one change), or ride the cheaper and faster bus 840 (see Buses on next page), either way is valid with a Bayern-Ticket (see next entry for details); **Munich** 2hr trip (2/hr, hrly from 5:45 until roughly 21:00), consider purchasing the Bayern-Ticket (explained below). **Note:** Because Salzburg is partnered with the German rail authority, special Deutsche Bahn train tickets (like the Bayern-Ticket) and Eurail passes that include Germany are valid to/fro Salzburg main train station at no additional cost. What's more, if you're traveling within Austria, purchase your ticket at least three days in advance and **save big** on the new **SparSchiene** fares! Go to the Austrian rail site (www.oebb.at), click English, enter your destination and departure date, click Book Ticket, then complete the correct number of passengers under 'Who is traveling?,' Calculate Fare, then compare trains and fares to find the right departure for you. By doing this, I've paid as little as 9€ one way from Salzburg to Innsbruck and 19€ from Salzburg to Vienna. Thus, there's no need to buy an Austrian Eurail pass anymore.

☞ The **Bayern-Ticket** is a terrific buy for individuals (23€) and small groups up to *five persons traveling for the day in 2nd-class seating within the German state of Bavaria and to/fro Salzburg main train station. (*The Bayern-Ticket costs an initial 23€ for the first person then add 5€ per person to a maximum of five persons, thus a two-person Bayern-Ticket costs 28€, three-person 33€, four-person 38€, five-person 43€.) Although the latter ticket is specifically aimed at Bavaria, it's ideal from Salzburg if you're headed across the German border to, for example, Munich or Berchtesgaden, which many of you will be. For instance, you can visit the Bavarian capital for the day, travel on the city's trams and buses and subway as needed, then return to Salzburg main train station for the aforesaid bargain price of 23€ one person or 28€-43€ for small groups up to five persons. For travel to Berchtesgaden, however, the Bayern-Ticket is not recommended for one person since the day ticket sold by the driver of bus 840 is a better deal (see Buses on next page). The Bayern-Ticket is also ideal for parents (and grandparents) who can use it to travel with an unlimited number of their own children (or grandchildren) aged 14 and under. What's more, there are many discounts on attractions Bavaria-wide afforded to holders of a valid Bayern-Ticket, in which case I've listed these where applicable throughout this guide, starting right here in the city of salt with a 10% discount on the Salzburg Card (page 9). **Note:** The Bayern-Ticket is valid Mon-Fri *after* 9:00 until 3:00 (the following morning) and the whole day Sat/Sun in 2nd-class seating on non-speed trains (heading to/fro Salzburg Hauptbahnhof across the German border) and on all public transportation within Bavaria (but *not* Salzburg) for the pocket-friendly price of 23€ one person or 28€-43€ for small groups up to five persons. But for this price the ticket must be purchased either online (www.bahn.de, print invoice and bring it on train with your credit card) or from the driver of bus 840 (headed to Berchtesgaden) or at a DB automat in Salzburg main train station (automats accept all major credit cards and are multilingual). To emphasize; if the ticket is bought over the counter you will pay a 2€ surcharge (i.e. 25€ for individuals and 30€-45€ for small groups), and even more if purchased on the train. The Bayern-Ticket is now available in the premier category of first-class seating (add roughly 12€ per person to the above-listed prices). Lastly, if you're holding a railpass, e.g. Eurail, you may not find the Bayern-Ticket such a bargain. Weigh your pass-type and destination against the price of the Bayern-Ticket.

ORIENTATION

Buses, (www.stadtbus.at). Salzburg isn't big enough to warrant a subway system, therefore an efficient and eco-friendly bus network (consisting of some 250 drivers operating 105 electric buses on 11 urban lines) does the trick. Most of the city's attractions can be found in the Old Town, or within walking distance of it, rendering public transportation for many travelers unnecessary. If you do require the service, however, the vast majority of my readers will be holding a valid Salzburg Card and therefore ride for free! Otherwise, the bus fares are: a **single** one-way ticket (Einzelkarte) costs 1.70€, or 2.50€ from driver. Youths 6-14yr buy the Einzelkarte "Minimum" ticket, .90¢ at automat or 1.30€ from driver. The **24-hour** ticket (24-Stundenkarte) 3.40€, or 5.50€ from driver, is good for exactly 24 hours from time of validation. Youths 6-14yr buy the 24-Stunden "Minimum" ticket, 1.70€ at automat or 2.80€ from driver. And the **week ticket** (Wochenkarte) 14.60€, not available for purchase from driver, is valid for exactly one week from first use and is transferable, meaning another person can use it. Purchase tickets at multilingual automats labeled Fahrkarten/Tickets or at magazine/tobacco shops. Tickets purchased from the bus driver are prevalidated but cost more money! Small groups consider hailing a cab. **Note:** Stamp ticket in time box on bus to validate; watch locals. An on-the-spot fine of 60€ will be enforced if caught riding Schwarz, i.e. without a valid ticket. To signal the driver to *stop* the bus, push button on handrail or by exit door. And note that at Mirabellplatz (one of Salzburg's main transportation hubs) there are three different pick-up points; check posted schedule to make sure you're in the right place.

    Bus 840 to Berchtesgaden (5.30€ one way, 50-min trip) departs typically Mon-Fri 8:15, 9:15, 10:15, 11:15, 13:05, 14:15, 15:15. 16:15, 17:15, 18:15, and Sat/Sun 9:15, 10:15, 11:15, 14:15, 15:15, 17:15 from opposite Salzburg's main train station (by "Forum 1" mall, or from *Mirabellplatz, Rathaus, and Mozartsteg a few minutes later. *Note that at Mirabellplatz there are three different pick-up points—you need to wait at the north end, i.e. the bus stop closest to main train station, but check schedule in advance for changes). If you're planning on returning to Salzburg, **purchase the day ticket** (Tageskarte adult 9.80€, youth 6-14yr 6.20€, family [2+2] 23€) from the driver, which will cover all your bus transportation for the day, including to/fro Salzburg and Obersalzberg (bus departure area for Eagle's Nest), as well as to the salt mines and Königssee lake (see my "Self-guided Berchtesgaden & Hitler's Eagle's Nest" guide). But if you are a **small group** of 4 or 5 persons, buy the Bayern-Ticket (explained on previous page) directly from the driver of bus 840 to significantly increase savings. Note that during the week (Mon-Fri) the Bayern-Ticket is officially valid *after* 9:00. The ticket is also valid Sat/Sun but there is neither an 8:15 bus nor an early time restriction on weekends. **Note:** Bus 840 terminates at Berchtesgaden's train station, where buses depart roughly every 30 min to Obersalzberg and elsewhere around town.

Getting to Berchtesgaden: This picturesque Bavarian village is only 25 km southwest of Salzburg (on the German side of the border) and, as you are probably already aware, highly worth a visit, especially mid-May thru October when the Eagle's Nest is open. From Salzburg you have five ways to reach Berchtesgaden: train, bus, taxi, car, pricey tour. **By train:** If you're holding a Eurail consecutive-day or dated Flexi/Select pass, you ride free on the train: 85-min trip (hrly with one change). **By bus:** If you're not holding a discounted rail pass (and even if you are you may want to) forget the train and ride bus 840 to Berchtesgaden. It's quicker and cheaper, (see entry above). **By taxi:** From Salzburg's main train station it will cost around 45€ to Berchtesgaden and 55€ to Obersalzberg. **By car:** Exit A10 autobahn at Salzburg-Süd and head direction Grödig; follow this road straight all the way (roughly 14 km). But if you're coming from central Salzburg, you need to get to the southeast side of town and connect onto the Alpenstrasse;

drive this straight to Berchtesgaden. **Pricey tour:** If interested, tours are available to Berchtesgaden from Salzburg; ask TI or staff at your digs for info.

Drivers/Parking:
For street parking pay at nearby automat and leave ticket on dashboard of your car (applicable Mon-Fri 9:00-19:00, Sat/Sun 9:00-16:00, otherwise free). Price (automat) typically 60¢/30 min, max 3.90€/3hr. There are a few **parking garages** around town, but the best choice for new arrivals is the 24-hour underground **Altstadt Garage** at Hildmannplatz 1 with 1,350 spaces available (1.20€/30 min, 2.40€/60 min, every 10 min thereafter 40¢, 18€/24hr, CCs ok, but note that many shops in the Old Town can discount your parking ticket to 4€/4hr or 6€/8hr if you make a purchase [thus ask about ticket validation before shopping], or Sporer spirits page 40 told me they would validate your parking ticket without having to purchase anything, just stop by and show this guide with your ticket). Getting to the Altstadt Garage is straightforward (GPS: N47 47.855 E13 02.264)—exit A1 autobahn at "Salzburg Flughafen" and follow signs to Salzburg, then Mitte and Hotel route. After about 4 km of winding through city streets you will reach a giant cliff face and a tunnel funneling into the Old Town—*don't* drive through the tunnel! A short distance before it, on the right, is the entrance descending to the garage. After parking, follow signs Festspielhäuser (Festival Halls page 20) to the Toskaninihof opening to the Old Town. (Sound of Music fans, both the Festival Halls and Toscanini Hof were used in the movie and are part of my DIY tour pages 86-88.) **Note:** That said, buy a beer and **park free** for the day at Müllner Bräu (page 42), found at Lindhofstrasse 7 north of the Old Town. Take ticket at gate and have beer cashier validate it.

Drivers who wish to **avoid the city** entirely, leave your car at the Salzburg Süd Park+Ride (nominal fee required) on the outskirts and ride the bus in. To get there, GPS: N47 46.150 E13 04.234, exit the A10 autobahn at Salzburg-Süd and continue in the direction of Salzburg—after about 4 km follow TI and Park+Ride (P+R) signs into parking lot. **Note:** Purchase Salzburg Card (page 9) from the on-site TI (see Tourist Information above for hours) and the bus ride into town is free as well as most attractions. As a reminder, vehicles traveling on the Austrian autobahn are required to have a "Vignette," or toll sticker (page 102).

The following examples of **traffic signs** can be commonly seen throughout Austria on its extensive network of roadways (for more traffic-sign examples, flip to page 103).

| Do not enter | Closed to all vehicles | One-way street | No parking | No parking or stopping |

Airport,
locally Flughafen (www.salzburg-airport.com; code: SZG; **free Wi-Fi** at airport—log on to "Freewave"; **free** viewing terrace at terminal 1). Salzburg's W.A. Mozart airport is idyllically nestled at the foothills of the Alps, which is a spectacular scene when flying to/fro the city of salt. Moving more than 1.5 million passengers annually, Salzburg airport is situated 5 km west of the Old Town with regular *bus connections or a **taxi** will cost roughly 15€ (depending on traffic and where you're headed); *daily bus #2 25 min to/fro main train station or Mirabellplatz, or bus #10 20 min to/fro the Old Town Rathaus or Hanuschplatz, adult 2.50€, youth 6-14yr 1.30€. **Note:** Consider purchasing the Salzburg Card; see info counter. Aviation aficionados, visit Hangar-7 (page 34) two bus stops (bus 2 direction city) from the main airport terminal.

ORIENTATION

Horse-Drawn Carriage, locally Fiaker. Romantic rides through the Old Town cost 44€/20-25 min or 88€/50 min, max 5 passengers. Carriages can readily be found on Residenzplatz (large gravel square punctuated by horse fountain), or if there's a festival in town they'll move to neighboring Domplatz (Cathedral Square). Note that rides double as a city tour, thus the better English your driver speaks the better your tour.

👍 **Salzburg Card:** I highly recommend you invest in the savings afforded by the Salzburg Card. You will not only gain un-limited use of public transportation within the metro area but also free one-time admission into most attractions (for example all sights in the do-it-yourself city orientation tour are free with the Salzburg Card), including select discounts on ser-vices and entertainment. The Salzburg Card comes in three validity types: 24, 48 and 72 hours (each available at the TI, airport info counter, and

possibly your accommodations). The cost of the card varies on the time of year (for example, the price increases May-Oct): **24-hour** card adult 24€, youth 6-15yr 12€ (May-Oct 27€/13.50€); **48-hour** card adult 32€, youth 6-15yr 16€ (May-Oct 36€/18€); **72-hour** card adult 37€, youth 6-15yr 18.50€ (May-Oct 42€/21€); TIs accept credit cards: VC, MC, DC; holders of a valid Bayern-Ticket receive a 10% discount on the Salzburg Card when purchased locally at the TI in the main train station. **Note:** The Salzburg Card is not valid until you sign and date it; do this prior to its first use.

Bike Rental: Salzburg is a pleasure to cycle around, and Top Bike will help you fulfill this eco-adventure. So get your butt in gear and ride your very own Tour de Salzburg. Cycle to Schloss Hellbrunn, along the river, or pedal my Sound of Music do-it-yourself Driving Tour (excluding lake district). Rent your wheels from Sabine at Top Bike (www.topbike.at, mobile 0676/476-7259)—show this guide and receive 20% off the below-listed prices. Top Bike is located on the old-town side of the Staatsbrücke (main bridge in town) and open daily (except in bad weather), April-June and Sept/Oct 10:00-17:00, July/Aug 9:00-19:00. Price (before discount), 6€/2hr, 10€/4hr, 15€/24hr, 45€/week. Bring ID.

Internet: Outside Salzburg's main train station you can pick up **free Wi-Fi** (log on to "Freewave" Mon-Sat till about 19:00) beaming from the "Forum 1" shopping mall (by McDonald's and Starbucks). If you prefer a computer terminal, use the shop just outside the station (3€/hr, daily 8:00-22:00). What's more, you can now pick up **free Wi-Fi** pro-vided by the city of Salzburg beaming in the Mirabell Gardens (by palace and "Do-Re-Mi" steps), riverbanks either side of the Makartsteg and Mozartsteg footbridges, at the Rathaus and on Mozartplatz in the Old Town under the moniker "Salzburg surf" (click "Einverstanden" to access) but surf time will be limited (www.salzburg-surft.at).

Post Office, Salzburg has three central branches: **(1)** Outside the main train station, between the Ramada hotel and Burger King, you'll find a P.O. (Mon-Fri 8:00-20:30, Sat 8:00-14:00, Sun 13:00-18:00). **(2)** The most centrally located P.O. (Mon-Fri 8:00-18:00) is hidden behind the cathedral, off Residenzplatz, at the same entrance as the Panorama Museum (page 14). **(3)** There's also a P.O. (Mon-Fri 8:00-18:30) at Schrannengasse 10, by the Mirabell Gardens.

Supermarket: A convenient and centrally located grocery store is the **Billa** (Mon-Fri 7:40-20:00, Sat 7:40-18:00, Sun 11:00-15:00) parked at the bus transportation hub Hanuschplatz, opposite the Makartsteg footbridge traversing the river. But a bigger stockpile of foodstuff can be found at the **EuroSpar** supermarket (all major CCs accepted, Mon-Fri 7:00-19:00, Sat 7:00-18:00, free Wi-Fi—log on to "Freewave") secreted in the "Forum 1" shopping mall outside the main train station. Open seven days a week, the new **Spar grocery store** (Mon-Sat 6:00-23:00, Sun 8:00-23:00) in the main train station often discounts its sandwich rolls by 50% late in the day (typically stocked next to the hot foods counter in front of you upon entering). On the New Town side of the river, a **Spar** grocery store (Mon-Fri 8:00-19:30, Sat 8:00-18:00) recently opened at Linzergasse 19.

Laundry: The only laundromat within walking distance of the Old Town is **Norge Exquisit Textilreinigung** (Mon-Fri 7:30-18:00, Sat 8:00-12:00, last wash two hours before closing, 14€/load, pay attendant), located at Paris-Lodron-Strasse 16 (on corner of Wolf-Dietrich-Strasse) in the New Town. North of the Old Town at Ignaz-Harrer-Strasse 32 is the coin laundry **Green & Clean** (daily 6:00-22:00, last wash 20:00, 10€/load); ride bus 2 to Gaswerkgasse.

What to do on a Sunday or holiday: The shops are closed but most all attractions will be open. At Mozartplatz, set off on my self-guided Salzburg tour (see next page). If you've been there done that, consider my Sound of Music do-it-yourself tour (page 82). If that's already checked off your list, head to Berchtesgaden, Werfen or the Salzkammergut (see Excursions page 64). Other ideas include renting a bike and cycling along the river or going for a hike (start with the Kapuzinerberg page 38). If none of the above appeals to you, how 'bout quaffing a beer or two under the cooling leaves of a chestnut tree at the Müllner Bräu (page 42).

Holidays in Salzburg, 2015

1. January, Thursday – Neujahr (New Year)
6. January, Tuesday – Heilige Drei Könige (Epiphany)
3. April – Karfreitag (Good Friday)
6. April – Ostermontag (Easter Monday)
1. May, Friday – May Day (Labor Day)
14. May, Thursday – Christi Himmelfahrt (Ascension Day)
25. May – Pfingstmontag (Whit Monday)
4. June, Thursday – Fronleichnam (Corpus Christi)
15. August, Saturday – Maria Himmelfahrt (Assumption Day)
26. October, Monday – National Independence Day
1. November, Sunday – Allerheiligen (All Saints' Day)
8. December, Tuesday – Immaculate Conception
25. December, Friday – Weihnachten (Christmas)
26. December, Saturday – St. Stephen's Day (Christmas Day 2)

Church Service, locally Gottesdienst. Note that hours may have changed; for the latest info and other religious denominations, check with staff at your digs or at the TI. **Roman Catholic** service in German is regularly held at the Dom (cathedral) Mon-Sat 6:30, Sun 8:30, *10:00 and 11:30 (*note the 10:00 service is often celebrated with choral music and the 11:00 service with organ music). **Holy Mass** in English is delivered twice monthly on the second and fourth Sunday at 17:00 at the Sacellum chapel, located opposite the Festspielhaus (corner of Hofstallgasse and Karajan-Platz). The **Evangelical service** in English, formerly held every Sunday at 11:00 in the Christuskirche, has moved to the suburb of Aigen—see TI for latest details or go to www.salzburgchurch.com.

FREE **SALZBURG**

(1) For an economical exploration of Salzburg, set off on my **self-guided tour**: Mozart-platz to Mirabell (see below). **(2)** To relive a movie classic, embark on the most popular outing in this guidebook: my **Sound of Music do-it-yourself tour** (page 82). Watch the movie free every evening at 19:00 at the hostel YoHo (page 52) or 20:00 at the JUFA hostel-hotel (page 53). **(3)** Capture a memorable view from the **Stein Terrasse** (page 38). **(4)** Though technically not without cost, the **Salzburg Card** (page 9) is mentioned here because it's such a good deal! In addition to umpteen discounts and freebies, present your Salzburg Card when booking the Mozart-Dinner-Concert (page 43) and receive the official concert CD absolutely free! **(5)** A trip to Salzburg wouldn't be complete without a stroll through the **Mirabell Gardens** (page 25); and within this magical open-air setting listen out for the free hour-long brass-band concerts held May-August every Wed 20:30 and Sun 10:30. **(6) Aviation aficionados** should visit Hangar-7 (page 34), an ultramodern structure housing vintage aircraft. **(7) Grave seekers** will find Mozart's wife Constanze and his father Leopold in St. Sebastian's Cemetery (page 32). **(8)** Hike the scenic and dramatic **Kapuzinerberg** (page 38).

DIY Old Town Tour

SIGHTS

Many of Salzburg's sightseeing attractions are listed within my 2-hour do-it-yourself orientation tour of the city (below). But if you only have enough time to visit one or two sights, the following is a short list of attractions and on which page to find them: Residenz (page 15), Cathedral (page 16), Fortress (page 17), St. Peter's Cemetery (page 18), Festival Halls (page 20), Old Market Square (page 21), Mozart's birthplace (page 22), river cruise ("boat ride" page 23), Mirabell Gardens (page 25), Mozart's second residence (Wohnhaus page 26), DomQuartier (page 28), Museum of Modern Art (page 31), Museum of Natural History (page 31), Schloss Hellbrunn (including trick fountains page 32), Salzburg Zoo (page 33), Brew World (page 34), Untersberg mountain cable car (page 35).

DO-IT-YOURSELF SALZBURG TOUR,
Mozartplatz to Mirabell—2 hours

You're fortunate, because today you are in Salzburg, one of Europe's most beautiful cities and my personal favorite. I had a guy once on one of my tours to Salzburg who, after each site we visited, said: "Just leave me here." I wasn't quite sure what he meant; maybe he wasn't happy with the tour, so I had to ask him if everything was okay. He replied: "Just leave me here, 'cause I never wanna go home."

You may not fall in love with Salzburg as this tourgoer did, but I do hope to at least educate, as well as entertain and inspire you during our walk together. So come on; let's discover Salzburg—Mozartplatz to Mirabell.

What's more, I've sprinkled this tour with sights made famous in the movie, "The Sound of Music." (Fans can combine this city tour with my SOM Walking Tour, page 86, by following the '**SOM fans**' notes included with each related entry.)

Note: Start early to maximize your time, between 9:00-10:00 is fine. (Tour is best April thru October, when flowers flourish and the Residenz fountain is *not* covered.) Wear comfy shoes; you have a fair bit of walking to do, enough to work off a super-sized strudel. **Allow at least two hours**; this does not include time spent touring the attractions. Note that all the attractions listed in this DIY tour are free with the **Salzburg Card** (page 9). You can buy the card at the TI where we start our tour on Mozartplatz. I suggest you walk with me through town to orient yourself then head back to sights of interest and begin using your card to maximize its value. Also, I'll point out **toilets** en route starting immediately with those at the Salzburg Museum (off Mozartplatz), and midway through the tour we bounce past a few **food options**: a casual eatery (before cemetery), an established restaurant (after cemetery), and a produce market (by Mozart's birthplace) recommended for a quick bite or a take-away picnic (to throw down in the Mirabell Gardens).

❶ (free Wi-Fi on square, "Salzburg surft," click "Einverstanden" to access): Ready? Let's begin on tourist-trampled **Mozartplatz** (GPS: N47 47.936 E13 02.873)

in front of the sizeable statue of the square's namesake, Wolfgang Amadeus Mozart. Although the statue is of considerable proportions, I find it unremarkable, liberally splattered in bird ca-ca and more akin to a resident of the Planet of the Apes than that of the legendary composer. And the pen clutched in his right hand looks like a Bic, which I'm certain did not exist in the 18th century. At the base of the statue (rear) is the year of its unveiling, 1842, stamped in Roman numerals. This is the same year Mozart's wife, Constanze Weber, died. We'll pass near her grave, together with Mozart's father Leopold, at the end of our tour.

As you gape at the imposing figure before you, ponder this: **Mozart**, child prodigy born in 1756, began playing the keyboard at the age of 3, wrote his first symphony at 8 and his first opera at 12. Mozart senior (Leopold) schlepped little Wolfgang around for months at a time during his youth to perform for the royal courts of Europe. During one of these tours, when Wolfgang was about 6, Leopold covered up the piano keys with a cloth to increase playing difficulty. Much to the astonishment of the crowd, Wolfgang tickled the ivories without missing a note. As an adult, Mozart favored the sophistication of Viennese culture over the intolerable holiness of small-town Salzburg. And so, in 1781, Mozart tired of composing "table music" on order of Salzburg's ruling archbishop and moved to Vienna, where he married Constanze Weber. Tragically, four of six children born to them died at birth or shortly thereafter. If things weren't depressing enough for the young couple, Mozart's lavish routine as a spendthrift brought more heartache in the form of poverty. In 1791, the prolific composer became ill and died on December 5, at the early age of 35. Except for the gravedigger and the priest, no one showed up for his funeral, not even his wife. A crestfallen rock star of his time, Wolfgang Amadeus Mozart was unceremoniously tossed into an unmarked commoner's grave (page 101) for a large amount of people.

And to think the musical maestro, lauded today as one of the greatest composers in history, was born only a few hundred meters from where you now stand. Perhaps he played in this very square as a child, that is, if he had the time.

Face the front of the statue; let's say Mozart is high noon (12:00) on a clock dial. To your left, at 10:00, is the **TI** (closed Sundays in Nov, otherwise daily 9:00-18:00, July thru mid-Sept till 19:00). Pick up a free map if you haven't already and, as mentioned above, consider buying the Salzburg Card (page 9).

Over your left shoulder, in the corner at 7:00, the plaza drops into **Judengasse**, or Jewish Lane. If you were to continue along this quaint shop-lined lane you'd first reach the unusual yet intriguing Easter-egg shop (page 40) then Mozart's birthplace a few minutes farther (which we'll visit later). But, for now, let's get back to his square and statue.

At 6:00, opposite Mozart and rising above his square, is the two-tone bell tower belonging to St. Michael's Church, dating from circa 800 A.D., thus making it one of the very first buildings constructed in Salzburg, but its current Baroque charm is owed to renovations in the mid-1700s.

DIY Old Town Tour

❶ Mozartplatz	❽ St. Peter's Cemetery	⓯ Mozart's Wohnhaus
❷ Salzburg Museum	❾ St. Peter's Church	⓰ Stein Terrasse
❸ Residenzplatz	❿ Festival Halls	Ⓐ Mönchsberg Lift
❹ Residenz	⓫ Old Market Square	Ⓑ Museum of Natural History
❺ Salzburg Cathedral	⓬ Mozart's Birthplace	Ⓒ Müllner Bräu
❻ Kapitelplatz	⓭ Boat ride & footbridge	Ⓓ Hotel Sacher
❼ Salzburg Fortress	⓮ Mirabell Gardens	Ⓔ Marionette Theater

❷ At 5:00 (in the direction Mozart is looking) is Residenzplatz (our next stop), and through the archway to Mozart's left is the **Salzburg Museum,** which opened June 2007 in the 400-year-old Neue Residenz, or New Residence, commissioned by Prince-Archbishop Wolf Dietrich as supplementary quarters to the Residenz (in the next square) to stroke his indulgent ego. During World War II, the Neue Residenz was appropriated by the Nazis as a command center. Postwar, the building was used by the U.S. Army as a regional headquarters until the early 1950s. Today, the city is the rightful owner and the aforementioned museum exhibits Salzburg's storied history, art and culture on multiple floors (www.salzburgmuseum.at, Tue-Sun 9:00-17:00, adult 7€, student 4€, youth 6-15yr 3€, family 14€, combo-ticket with Panorama Museum 8.50€/4.50€, or free with Salzburg Card, audio guide included with admission, allow at least 60 min for a visit; on the upper floor are terrific views of the Old Town; scenic café on first floor; kids receive fun passport-like document to stamp at the various Kinder Welt, or Kid's World, exhibits).

Military buffs allow at least 30 minutes to browse one of the museum's current exhibitions, a gripping look at Salzburg and its citizenry during World War One. The exhibition runs through Sept 27, 2015 and is displayed in English across the first floor.

Another part of the museum's collection, but rarely on display due to its sensitivity to light, is the oldest known sheet music of the Christmas carol "Silent Night" penned by Joseph Mohr (circa 1820) in the town of Oberndorf (page 64).

To find the museum's free and clean **toilets,** step straight through the archway and again through its main entrance in front of you, go right and down the stairs one level.

Connected to the Salzburg Museum is the **Panorama Museum,** a large bi-level room exhibiting a series of painted city and landscapes (as seen in the 19th century, from Moscow to New York and the Matterhorn to the Grand Canyon) called cosmoramas that bound the museum's namesake "panorama." Majestic and magnificent, the panorama painted by J.M. Sattler is an enormous 130-square-meter cyclorama, or circular mural, of Salzburg as viewed from the fortress' lookout tower in the year 1829. Upon the panorama's completion, Sattler and his family toured Europe with it for 10 years (1829-39). At each destination, from Oslo to Prague, the panorama was displayed in a pavilion so its residents could marvel the beauty of Salzburg, often billed as the "Rome of the north" because of its myriad piazzas and church steeples. After the Sattlers returned home, Salzburg exhibited the panorama, along with the cosmoramas, permanently in its own tribute pavilion near the Mirabell Gardens until 1937. Today, Sattler's panorama has been lovingly restored (exceeding 4,400 work hours) and is now on display for you to admire in this purpose-built museum (for hours, admission and panorama viewing pointers, see page 28).

(**SOM fans,** in the next paragraph we bid farewell to Mozart, but before *you* do, walk behind the statue and angle left downhill to the river. Cross with the traffic light and take a quick trip across the **Mozart Steg** footbridge, see page 91, then return here and...)

▶ Bid farewell to Mozart—it's only temporary though, because I'll show you where he was born a bit later on—and start walking in the direction of 5:00 to the graveled Residenzplatz and stand by the fountain. En route, a striking but brief view of the fortress will present itself on the left. Also on the left, beneath the clock tower, is the fabric store Salzburger Heimatwerk. (If you're interested in a traditional pair of lederhosen, a maiden's dirndl or dressmaking materials, see page 39.) Beyond Heimatwerk is the post office (Mon-Fri 8:00-18:00) together with the main entrance into the Panorama Museum.

❸ Marking the heart of **Residenzplatz** is Residenz fountain. Dating from 1658, it is said to be the most beautiful Baroque fountain north of the Alps. Fans of the movie "The Sound of Music" will recognize it as the fountain Maria splashes water in the horse's face while singing "I Have Confidence." (She splashed the horse facing the Hypo building, blue logo. Note that the fountain is covered for winter, typically  from early Nov until the end of March. If this is your time frame, you now have an excuse to come back.) Residenzplatz, or Residence Square, is the largest square in town. It is the scene of Salzburg's Christmas market, a number of festivals throughout the year and occasionally the venue for big-time concerts, like the time in June 2000 when I stood here with 10,000 other cheering fans watching Eddie Vedder front Pearl Jam. Other names who have performed here are Neil Young, Simply Red, and Eros Ramazzotti. In recent years, A-list artists such as Elton John, Joe Cocker and Mark Knopfler have performed in Salzburg, but event management now hosts its stars in the contemporary 6,700-seat Salzburgarena—check Web or TI for latest listings.

👆 Look back to the New Residence; you now have an up-close view of its high-flying bell tower, or **Glockenspiel.** Dating from 1703, the Glockenspiel's 35 chiming bells once admired by Mozart now play Mozart tunes thrice daily: 7:00, 11:00, 18:00. **Note:** If you're in town on a Thursday (17:30) or Friday (10:30), April-Oct, join the recommended **Glockenspiel tour** (adult 3€, student/senior 60yr+ 2€, youth 6-15yr 1.50€; Salzburg Card not valid; reserve your spot in advance with cashier at Salzburg Museum). Know that on this 30-minute tour you'll need to climb more than 100 calorie-burning steps to reach the tower's narrow observation terrace (if you have a fear of heights, like me, go at least as far as the clock mechanism then see if you can manage the few remaining steps to the viewing platform. I did it. I was petrified, but I did it).

❹ Residenzplatz takes its name from the **Residenz,** the prominent building on the square (opposite Glockenspiel) with three rows of windows stacked one on top of the other. Established in 1102 and enlarged during the 17th-18th centuries, the Residenz is the former state rooms and living quarters of Salzburg's powerful prince archbishops, men who were inspired by Rome and the pope. Alas, much of the original furniture did not survive the cravings of Napoleon's troops in the 1800s or the Habsburgs who chronologically followed. The city has done a superb job of restoring the Residenz to its former glory (thus I

recommend you tour it if time is on your side; for hours and admission see **DomQuartier** page 28). It was here (in the Konferenz Saal, room 4) that Mozart played his first court concert (in front of Prince-Archbishop Schrattenbach) at the age of 6; where Leopold Mozart was portrayed in the movie "Amadeus" asking the archbishop to retrieve his son from Vienna; and where Emperor Franz I on May 1, 1816, administered the oath of allegiance to the Salzburg trades, officially incorporating Salzburg into Austria.

Right of the Residenz opens into Alter Markt, or Old Market Square, which we'll visit later. At this right corner, on the Residenz's side wall (almost directly opposite the Jahn-Markl store), is a wooden display case notifying passersby of the daily tunes played by the Glockenspiel.

Left of the Residenz, through the arches, leads onto Domplatz, our next stop. Above the arches is a skywalk formerly connecting the archbishops with the Dom, or cathedral, so they could avoid commoners on the way to Mass.

DIY Old Town Tour

In front of the Residence, **horse-drawn carriages** (called Fiaker) patiently wait for the pleasure to trot you through the Old Town (44€/20-25 min or 88€/50 min, max 5 passengers). Because rides double as a city tour, interested parties should request a driver who speaks reasonable English before setting off.

▶ Stroll through the arches into Domplatz, the square facing the cathedral. Along the way you are unknowingly crossing a former excavation site. A testament to the city's prosperity, some 55 years ago archaeologists discovered a trove of artifacts and ruins dating from the medieval cathedral to as far back as Roman times when Salzburg was known as Iuvavum. Beneath the **left arch** is a stairwell descending below ground where you can explore the Domgrabungsmuseum, or cathedral excavations (July/Aug daily 9:00-17:00, closed remainder of year, adult 2.50€, student 1.50€, or free with Salzburg Card. Although fascinating for archaeologist-types, the general traveler will find the excavations hard to decipher).

At the **right arch** say "Hi" to my artist friend, Igor Zindovic (pictured), who has been parked here since the mid-1990s painting and selling his artwork. Show Igor this guidebook and he'll give you a deal along with a big dose of friendly conversation.

❺ 👍 From Domplatz (Cathedral Square) we have a divine view of the city's premier house of God, the Salzburger Dom, or **Cathedral** (visiting hours Mon-Sat 8:00-17:00, Sun 13:00-17:00, March/April & Oct daily till 18:00, May-July & Sept daily till 19:00, August daily till 20:00, donations welcome. For Mass times, see Church Service on page 10. If time is on your side, tour the adjoining **Cathedral Museum** now part of the **DomQuartier** page 28).

The Salzburger Dom is the largest Baroque structure north of the Alps, having the capacity to hold more than 10,000 of us. Fittingly, Mozart was baptized here in 1756 (in font left of entry), and the "Hoforgel" organ inside (right) he often played. But before you enter its holy domain, waddle into the middle of the plaza, stand by the statue of the Virgin Mary and face the cathedral. Above its wrought-iron gates are three landmark dates in the Dom's history: <u>774</u>, consecration of original structure (long since ruined). <u>1628</u>, rebuilt in the Baroque-style you see today and reconsecrated (after cathedral was destroyed by fire in the late 16th century). <u>1959</u>, reconstructed after Allied bombs shattered it during World War II (pictures inside cathedral, back left, depict this blasphemous day). Flanking the gates are four figures, (left to right): **St. Rupert** (founder of Salzburg/patron saint of salt), **St. Peter** (holder of the keys to Heaven), **St. Paul** (holding a sword—assumed beheaded by Romans), and **St. Virgil** (first archbishop of Salzburg and creator of the Dom).

Atop the cathedral is a statue of Jesus, flanked by Moses (left) and Elijah (right). Midway up the facade you'll see the four evangelists: John, Paul, George and Ringo. Um, err, I mean Matthew, Mark, Luke and John. Just above them are two angels holding a crown. Now, walk beyond the Virgin Mary in the direction she is facing and stand beneath the middle archway. Once there, line up Mary's head under the angels. When ready, pace forward and the angels crown her. Neat, huh?

While facing the cathedral **look for Vlado** (pictured), another of my artist friends whom I've known for many years; he is usually standing immediately right of the entrance (April-May & July-Aug, 11:00-18:00 but not in bad weather). He'll masterfully cut out your portrait like Edward Scissorhands on high-octane turnip juice (4€, but show Vlado this guide and pay 3€. If he doesn't give you the discount, the artist is not Vlado)!

❻ When ready, continue right past the cathedral through the *arches and into the next square, Kapitelplatz, where you'll be graced with a so-close-you-can-almost-reach-upwards-and-touch-it view of the fortress and Stephan Balkenhol's larger-than-life man on golden globe (called "Sphaera," erected in 2007). To your immediate left is arguably **Europe's largest chess set** (board painted onto asphalt), with pieces the size of children. If you care to play, notify the regu-

lator (person who appears informed) that you're up for the challenge. On your right are souvenir stands laden with Mozart mementos, useless knickknacks, scenic postcards, and T-shirts with catchy print like 'No Kangaroos in Austria.'

*If you have the urge, **toilets** (WC) can be found at the arches (bring small change for stall, 50¢). On Kapitelplatz beams **free Wi-Fi**, "Salzburg surf," click "Einverstanden" to access).

❼ 👆 One reason people like myself absolutely adore Salzburg is its history; it's downright mind-boggling! A good example is the massive structure in front of you. Lording over the city for more than 900 years, stark and imposing, the **Fortress of Salzburg** is every bit the castle I envisioned while listening to fairy tales as a child. And here it is, perched upon a forested bluff in western Austria, flexing its muscles; an impregnable curtain of stonework and turrets. Dating from 1077 A.D., Salzburg's fortress (Festung Hohensalzburg) was never conquered, and today it registers as one of the largest fully preserved castle complexes in Europe. It is the city's signature landmark, where the ruling archbishops resided before moving downtown to the Residenz. Needless to say, this must-explore fortress site is highly worth your time (and free with the Salzburg Card, including the cable railway you see lifting visitors to its ramparts—allow at least two hours for a fortress visit—for opening times, admission, and audio-guide tour, see page 29).

▶ Continue straight through the square; we're headed up the cobbled lane running between the buildings. But before we go that route, I want you to veer right and slip through the corner wrought-iron gate (one of three entrances into St. Peter's Cemetery). Inside on the left is **Salzburg's oldest bakery** (and probably its smallest, Mon-Tue & Thur-Fri 8:00-17:30, Sat 7:00-13:00, closed Wed). It belongs to St. Peter's monastery (which we'll soon visit) and has been baking bread in a wood-fired oven here since the 12th century.

Today, the bread is baked mornings from 4:00 till 7:00; an on-site exhibit illustrates how it's done. For something to nibble on during our tour, consider buying a bread roll similar to rye (.80¢), sourdough (half kg 2€), or perhaps a sweet raisin-roll (1€). (Note that later we'll be walking through an outdoor market selling various meats and cheeses that sandwich well with the bread.)

The adjacent **surging waterway** (called the Almkanal, typically shut down late September for maintenance) has been flowing in from Germany since medieval times and was an integral part of the city's water supply as well as a canal system used to flush the filth from the streets, power grain mills, and (of course) sustain the bakery.

Retrace your steps back out the wrought-iron gate and go right up the cobbled lane (Festungsgasse) toward the fortress. Ahead on the right is a **casual eatery** (daily 10:00-17:00, summer till 20:00) affording its guests reasonable prices, a picture menu, and an ivy-blanketed patio-garden with fortress view. The hard-working owner, Helmut, dishes up his locally famed two-course lunch special consisting of soup, schnitzel and potatoes (Kartoffel) for 8.90€. Adjoining the eatery is a souvenir shop managed by Alex, who's worked here for about as long as I've been guiding groups through Salzburg, since 1998.

Beyond the mementos and Mozart chocolates is another wrought-iron gate leading into St. Peter's Cemetery, our next stop. But before we venture through said gate, I first want to point out the **cable railway** (Festungsbahn) in front of you climbing to the fortress, the most expedient way up; (note there are free **toilets** inside the railway entrance). And if you were to continue up the cobbled lane you'd soon reach the restaurant **Stieglkeller** (page 46), then beyond it a crossroads: right climbs steeply to the fortress, straight leads to the Nonnberg abbey.

> (**SOM fans**, flip to page 89 and above the Untersberg entry read from "At the top the lane splits direction…." and finish after the Nonnberg abbey entry.)

❽ ✌ Mosey through the gate into **St. Peter's Cemetery** (daily 6:30-18:00, April-Sept till 19:00), the oldest active graveyard in Austria, and world famous for hiding the Trapp family in "The Sound of Music." (Actually, Hollywood hid the von Trapps in a studio but this cemetery inspired the director. **SOM fans**, flip to page 88 to find the real Max Detweiler.) St. Peter's Cemetery is a mix of old and new graves linked via lopsided footpaths and encompassed by a succession of vaulted burial chambers belonging to titled families. Vault **XVI**, for example, belongs to Lorenz Hagenauer, landlord to the Mozart family (Getreidegasse address); and within vault **XXXI** is the architect Santino Solari, famous for building the cathedral, Schloss Hellbrunn, and many of Salzburg's

fortifications constructed during the Thirty Years' War. In the center of the graveyard is **St. Margaret's chapel**, the only church in Salzburg that still stands as it did in the 15th century (1491). It's amazing to think that Europeans were already building cathedrals, fighting wars, and brewing beer long before my country was even a twinkle in our forefathers' eyes. (If the entrance to St. Margaret's is shut, the interior may be viewed through two peepholes in the main portal.) Framing the chapel, plots dressed in a symphony of multihued flowers are immaculately tended, most burning a red remembrance candle, breaking the black stillness of the night. Meters from the water basin in the center of the cemetery—

coins thrown in from well wishers regularly cleaned by entrepreneurial vagabonds—is the plot of U.S. Major General **Harry J. Collins**, commander of the distinguished 42nd Infantry "Rainbow" Division (Seventh Army) from July 1943 thru May '45. After the war, Collins was promoted to military governor of U.S. forces in Austria. It was during this time that he fell in love with Salzburg and one of its offspring, Irene Gehmacher. The general died in the early '60s and is buried here with his wife. His headstone reads: "Honorary citizen of the cities of Salzburg and Linz." Behind the general's grave (against the church wall), ironically, is a memorial dedicated to the Axis soldiers who fell in defense of the city during the war.

Going back a few years, before the general and World War II, are the so-called "catacombs" in the cliff face. These are dwellings dug out by Christians during the days of the Romans in the third century A.D. At its entrance are the graves of **Mozart's sister**—Maria Anna (a.k.a. Nannerl)—and Michael Haydn, a celebrated composer in Salzburg and brother to the "father of the symphony," Joseph Haydn.

On page 30 I've penned a **do-it-yourself tour** for you through the catacombs. Either come back later for a visit or whip out your Salzburg Card and tour the dugouts now—it'll only take 15-20 min.

❾ Exit the cemetery via the arched passageway (beneath church clock tower) and into the next plaza.

You are now standing in the courtyard of **St. Peter's (Benedictine) monastery**, the oldest community of monks in the German-speaking world (in which some 30 are still active), and where Bishop Rupert founded Salzburg more than 1,300 years ago. Thus it's not surprising that St. Peter's Stiftskeller (to your left) is **Europe's oldest restaurant!** The Stiftskeller was first mentioned in the year 803 by the court scribe Alcuin during a visit by the great Emperor Charlemagne. It is likely the Stiftskeller, or monastic cellar managed by the church, was the monks' regular buffet decades prior to the emperor's visit and therefore much older. Although the prices have increased since then (16€-27€ main dish, all major CCs accepted, English menu available, daily, page 46), I recommend you stop in sometime for a bite to eat, even if it's only for a soup, dessert or dinner concert (see Mozart-Dinner-Concert page 43).

✍ The Stiftskeller faces another of Salzburg's pious landmarks, **St. Peter's Church.** Built between 1130-1143, St. Peter's lavish renovations during the Baroque and Rococo periods (17/18th centuries) have transformed the interior of this must-see church into the region's most spectacular. In 1789, Mozart directed his Dominicus Mass in C-minor here while his wife, Constanze, sang soprano. It is within this

DIY Old Town Tour

hallowed structure that Bishop Rupert is buried. Look for the "Grab des Hl. Rupertus" midway along the right aisle.

▶ Continuing our platz hop, saunter across the square, paralleling the sheer cliffs that cradle the fortress, and <u>stop</u> beneath the next arched passage. Here you have a memorable view of the church, square, fountain, restaurant and fortress. Snap!

Sashay straight through the passage and into the adjoining courtyard, home to the College of St. Benedict for aspiring monks. Mozart's father, Leopold, studied here for a short while (before he excused himself on account of his love for music). Pass a welcoming Bishop Rupert (patron saint of salt) with a drum of the "white gold" at his feet, and head through the next passage into the Toscanini Hof (**SOM fans** see page 88), a secluded courtyard named after the distinguished Italian conductor, Arturo Toscanini (1867-1957).

To your left, a passageway cuts through the cliff face into the underground **Altstadt Garage**, the ideal parking lot for daytrippers (for more info on the garage, see Parking page 8). During World War II, the garage was used as an air-raid shelter. It was also here that initial talks took place leading to the surrender of Salzburg after its liberation on May 4, 1945 from the Nazis by "dog-faced soldiers" of the U.S. 3rd Infantry "Marne" Division. (The plaque affixed to the stone wall right of the passageway tells the story.)

In front of you is the House for Mozart, the south end of Salzburg's renowned festival halls. Through its massive iron doors stage crews regularly wrestle with the loading and unloading of hefty props and technical equipment for the latest productions.

From here the festival halls appear to be rather insignificant. But let's make tracks and get a significant view. To your right is an underpass, roll through this and <u>stop</u> in the middle of the street (Max-Reinhardt-Platz), mindful of the horse dung left by the procession of Fiakers clip-clopping tourists around town.

(Shortly, we'll keep going straight and take the lane running alongside the domed church, but first I want to point out a few sites:) Look right. Do you recognize anything? The far archway is on the edge of Domplatz, where you lined up the angels to crown the Virgin Mary. Now turn around; the enormous building you see extending the entire length of the block accommodates Salzburg's grand festival halls. If you were to walk a few minutes beyond the halls, paralleling the cliffs, you'd reach the **Ⓐ Mönchsberg Lift** (page 31), elevators which access the Mönchsberg observation terrace, one of Salzburg's most scenic vantage points and where (**SOM fans** will be interested to know) Maria and the kids sang "Do-Re-Mi." Adjoining the terrace is the **Museum of Modern Art** (page 31, beige building with castle-like turret), and just down the street from the base of the Lift (towards the river) is the **Ⓑ Museum of Natural History** (page 31 — fun for kids!).

❿ Festival Halls, locally Festspielhäuser, (<u>GPS</u>: N47 47.904 E13 02.569), a massive 17th-century structure formerly the archbishop's stables and riding school. The **large festival hall**, or Grosses Festspielhaus, impressive in its size (at the north end of the complex), has seating for 2,200 of us and is outfitted with one of Europe's largest opera stages, totaling 100 meters in width. The second largest theater, **Haus für Mozart** (at the south end of the building), dates from 1924 and recently underwent a three-year, 29€-million renovation for the 250-year celebration of Mozart's birth. The so-called **Summer Riding School**, or Felsenreitschule, is the most historic venue, dating from 1693 when the archbishop's horses trained and performed here. This striking theater has seating for 1,400 guests beneath a state-of-the-art retractable roof that can open on the flip of a switch (depending on the scene) and features three dramatic tiers of stone arcades hewn into the cliff face (pictured) that moviegoers will recognize in "The Sound of Music" when the Hollywood von Trapps sing "Edel-weiss" before escaping to the cemetery.

The only way to visit the Festival Halls, besides paying 50€-500€ to see a performance, is by taking the recommended 45-minute mul-tilanguage tour. (For Sound of Music fans, the tour is a must! Turn to page 86 for more SOM movie trivia regarding the halls.) **Tours** of the Festival Halls (adult 6€, youth 6-12yr 3€, or free with Salzburg Card) run daily (times may change due to events or theater perfor-mances) and meet at the Festival ticket shop (by iron gate and column with mask atop 15 min prior to the following times): Oct-May at 14:00; June and Sept at 14:00 & 15:30; July/Aug 9:30, 14:00 & 15:30. The world-famous **Salzburg Festival** (Salzburger Festspiele) this year is scheduled from July 18 thru August 30, 2015. For tickets and info, either go to the Festival Halls box office, the Mozartplatz TI, or online: www.salzburgfestival.at.

▶ Take the lane (Wiener-Philharmoniker-Gasse) running alongside the domed church to the **open-air victuals market**, an animated place to gather lunch (Mon-Fri early till

around 18:00, Sat till around 15:00). Choose from a variety of meats, cheeses, fruits, vegetables, pretzels, and grilled sausages, locally Würste. (**SOM fans**, re-member the scene when Maria juggled the tomatoes and Gretl dropped hers? It was filmed right here on **University Platz**.)

To your right (before first food stand), look to the plaque above the Restaurant Zipfer. It reads, "In this house lived W. A. Mozart's sister Nannerl (widowed baroness von Berchtold zu Sonnenburg) from October 28, 1801 until her death October 29, 1829."

Speaking of Wolfgang Amadeus, we began this tour on his square, Mozartplatz, and since then you've learned a few things about the master composer. Now, you're within a pretzel toss of where the master was born. Look to the golden facade in front of you; this is the back of Mozart's birthplace. We'll arrive at its front facade in about 15 minutes; first I want to show you Salzburg's most senior market square.

When ready, go right through the tall, arched passage. Midway through is a petite shop selling the sugary satisfaction of Fürst confectionery, dutifully supervised by the sepia eyes of its founder, Paul Fürst (see Mozart Balls page 39). The next shop along, on the corner, is Austria's oldest bookstore, since 1594 (Mon-Fri 9:00-18:30, Sat 9:00-18:00); you'll find its English-language section against the left wall.

Continue straight to the next platz, Alter Markt. (If class is in session, you'll pass an eclectic string of bicycles parked in front of the historic university building, housing the criminal justice department.) Once in the plaza turn left, <u>stop</u>, and face the flag-bearing statue (Florian fountain).

⓫ After leveling the charred houses destroyed by the fire of 1262, the townsfolk decided to build an expansive firebreak to better protect the inner-city residents and their dwell-ings from a future inferno. So came about Alter Markt, or **Old Market Square,** where locals flocked in medieval times to buy and sell their goods.

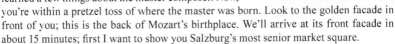

In the center of the square is **Florian fountain**, the neighborhood's former water supply, capped by the saint himself, patron of fire protection, depicted in action pouring a bucket of water over a burning castle.

To your left is **Café Tomaselli** (page 50), Austria's oldest coffeehouse, dating from 1703, where Mozart played cards while contentedly consuming cake and caffeine. Also a regular visitor, Constanze Weber (Mozart's widow) lived above the café from 1820-26 with her second husband. More importantly, pay **toilets** can be found inside Tomaselli's, straight to the back, up the stairs.

Across the square from Café Tomaselli is **Café Fürst** (page 49), another of Salzburg's authentic coffee institutions and home of the original Mozart chocolate ball. Right of Café Fürst you'll recognize graveled Residenzplatz.

Left of the fountain, or third doorway from Café Tomaselli, is **Salzburg's smallest house** (2.2 m wide x 8 m long), dating from 1860, built in a former alleyway. It's not much of a house, more like a gap between two buildings. Add a door, a window, throw on a few tiles for a roof, nail in a gargoyle and call it the smallest house in town. Ha!

Right of Florian fountain is the city's oldest **pharmacy** (Apotheke), dating from 1591, still in operation today (Mon-Fri 8:00-18:00, Sat 8:00-12:00). Two doors along is a sweets shop parading chocolate in its front window. Boxes upon boxes, in all shapes and sizes, filled with little chocolate balls wrapped in shiny foil. Compare Fürst's original **Mozart ball** (page 39) with the competition's imitation blend.

Skip to the lower end of the square and stop. To your right begins Judengasse. Do you remember this Jewish Lane that leads to decorated Easter eggs and Mozartplatz?

Jog left. This leads to **Getreidegasse** (pictured), meaning Grain Lane, Salzburg's main shopping street, teeming with tourists buzzing beneath a multitude of gilded wrought-iron signs hanging over retail outlets.

Follow the crowds a short distance to the rich-yellow facade at number 9, Mozart's birthplace, looking much like it did in his day, minus the fan frenzy. Right of its entrance portal, notice the building's original doorbells. The middle one jingled the Mozart's apartment.

⑫ **Mozart's birthplace,** locally Geburtshaus, (GPS: N47 48.011 E13 02.617). The legendary "Amadeus," baptized as Johannes Chrysostomus Wolfgangus *Theophilus Mozart, was born January 27, 1756 in the apartment on the third floor of this six-story dwelling in the heart of the Old Town at Getreidegasse 9 (pictured, now a museum, www.mozarteum.at, allow 25 min for a visit, climb 20 steps to cashier, daily 9:00-17:30 last entry 17:00, July/Aug 8:30-19:00 last entry 18:30, adult 10€, student/senior 8.50€, youth 6-14yr 3.50€ & 15-18yr 4€, family 21€, combo-ticket with Wohnhaus available, or free with Salzburg Card).

*Amadeus, as he is so often referred to, comes from Theophilus, which translates to Gottlieb in German, Amadeus in Latin, and "beloved by God" in English. He routinely used Wolfgang Amadeus as his signature and is therefore generally known by these two names.

Wolfgang was the seventh and last child born to Leopold and Anna Maria Mozart. The parents moved into this third-floor apartment in 1747, where they lived for 26 years before relocating across town in 1773 (to the Wohnhaus page 26). The Getreidegasse apartment is quite small, consisting of a kitchen, foyer, living room, bedroom and study. Within these tight confines, Anna Maria gave birth seven times; only two survived infancy. In 1751, Wolfgang's sister, Maria Anna (a.k.a Nannerl), was born and five years later came Amadeus. Mozart's birth room (Geburtszimmer) is the third one after entering

the exhibition. It is here the musical maestro penned many of his first compositions, thus it is an absolute treat to eyeball the very clavichord and petite violin Mozart played as a youngster. Also in the museum you'll discover original family documents, paintings and personal belongings, as well as a lock of Mozart's hair. (Inset: graphic of a 55-cent postage stamp released in January 2006 by the Deutsche Post to commemorate Mozart's 250th birthday.)

▶ Continue along Getreidegasse some 50 meters to the archway at No. 24 (right). Stop here. We're headed through this passageway but if you were to continue straight along Getreidegasse to No. 33 (left) you would reach Salzburg's **best curry sausages** (page 50) and six doors farther at No. 39 you'd strike the lane's narrowest house and a Salzburg tradition, **Sporer wines & spirits** (page 40). When the time is right, step inside and taste test Sporer's essential orange punch, prepared according to a secret recipe handed down from grandfather Otto.

March through the portal at No. 24, straight down the passageway and out the other end. You're now at bustling **Hanuschplatz**, a major transportation hub where environmentally friendly buses repetitively transfer commuters here and there. For example, you could pick up bus 1 (from across the street) to **Stiegl's Brew World** (page 34), or to shop with locals at the **Europark mall** (page 41), or ultimately to the **casino** (page 36) to possibly win a fortune. More bus connections depart from "Rathaus" a short jog to your right up the street.

Swing left to the crosswalk (if you didn't get all you wanted back at the victuals market, you can usually find it here on the left at the **Billa grocery store:** Mon-Fri 7:40-20:00, Sat 7:40-18:00, Sun 11:00-15:00).

Cross the street, then once again, to the river. Left of the footbridge (called Makartsteg) you'll see the dock for Salzburg's one-and-only panorama boat that cruises tourists up and down the river.

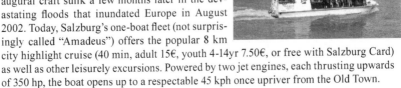

🄑 In 2002, Salzburg built a dock for visitors craving a Schifffahrt, or **boat ride,** on the Salzach River—the first time since 1891. Fatefully, the inaugural craft sunk a few months later in the devastating floods that inundated Europe in August 2002. Today, Salzburg's one-boat fleet (not surprisingly called "Amadeus") offers the popular 8 km city highlight cruise (40 min, adult 15€, youth 4-14yr 7.50€, or free with Salzburg Card) as well as other leisurely excursions. Powered by two jet engines, each thrusting upwards of 350 hp, the boat opens up to a respectable 45 kph once upriver from the Old Town.

DIY Old Town Tour

River cruises depart hourly March 27 thru Nov 1, 2015 (no departures outside these dates): daily **March** 27 thru **April,** 15:00-16:00 except weekends from 13:00; **May** 11:00-17:00; **June** 11:00-18:00; **July** 11:00-19:00; **Aug** 1-15 11:00-20:00; **Aug** 16-31 11:00-19:00; **Sept** 12:00-17:00; **Oct** thru **Nov** 1 13:00 & 15:00-16:00. In peak season, mid-June thru Aug, pick up your ticket(s) in advance from the operator's on-site kiosk. Consider the excursion (Tour II) to Schloss Hellbrunn and the zoo (free with Salzburg Card, ride bus back into town)—see operator for departure times. Note: During summer, seats on the back deck are allocated for a fee.

▶ By way of the footbridge, cross the river, locally called the Salzach, or Salt River, not because of any salt content but for the river trade in medieval times that transported the "white gold" downstream from the **salt mines** at nearby Dürrnberg (page 37) via the Inn and Danube rivers, eventually the Black Sea and into the coffers of powerful Asian rulers. Much closer, 20 km downstream, the Salt River flows through the border town of **Oberndorf** (page 64), home to the Christmas carol "Silent Night."

(You just departed the left bank of Salzburg, or Old Town, and are now headed to its right bank, or New Town, named because of the city's recent mass expansion across the river in the 18th century.)

On the bridge you noticed the crazy amount of **padlocks** attached to the cable fenc-

ing. This ardent craze has spread across European bridges with gusto over the last years. You see, young lovers fasten their engraved padlock to the bridge and toss the key over the side, into the river below to symbolize their eternal union to one another. Now you know the story of the myriad padlocks, perhaps it's a bond you'd like to make with your partner? (If you're reading this in advance of your trip, have a padlock custom engraved—with both your first names and the date your relationship was consummated—and surprise your significant other by attaching it to the bridge while in Salzburg. You can thank me later! If you're reading this while already on the road, ask a local where you can buy a padlock and get it engraved.)

Stop at the midway point of the bridge to take in the stupendous view of Salzburg Old Town. Vying for attention against the backdrop of its landmark fortress crowning the skyline, stylized steeples stand tall like a pageant of beauty queens above immense churches wittingly built by ruling archbishops to showcase their divine authority.

Look downstream: the copper-topped church steeple you see rising from the hillside belongs to the Augustinian monastery, home to Austria's largest tavern and beer garden, ❻ **Müllner Bräu** (page 42).

Turn around and look upstream to the neighboring, motor-trafficked bridge. Facing it (from New Town) is the Hotel Stein, where we'll end our tour on its scenic rooftop café, Stein Terrasse (page 38).

Mosey down the latter half of the footbridge and onto the right bank. The elongated structure on the right is the ❼ 5-star **Hotel Sacher** (page 58). In 1964, Julie Andrews and director Robert Wise stayed here during the filming of "The Sound of Music." Besides stately digs, Sacher is known for its rich chocolate torte. Yum. On the way past, consider picking up a Würfel (mouth-sized piece 3.30€) at the classy Sacher sweets shop (straight ahead and through door on right, Mon-Fri 9:30-18:00, Sat 9:30-17:00).

(**Picnickers**, a choice place to enjoy your goodies is along the riverbank—bench or grass—or wait a few minutes until we reach our next stop, the Mirabell Gardens.)

Continue straight ahead. At the traffic intersection, cross with the light (left cross-walk) and <u>stop</u> on the forward corner. We're going to keep walking straight (away from river) but if you were to go left, the next building along is the **E** **Marionette Theater** (page 44). It was these puppets that inspired the Lonely Goatherd sequence in the "The Sound of Music."

Keep walking straight and <u>stop</u> on the other side of the Landestheater (meaning Provincial Theater). In front of you is the 5-star Hotel Bristol, where the remainder of "The Sound of Music" cast stayed during filming. To your right, across the street, the corner building is Mozart's Wohnhaus (the family's second residence). We'll head over there in a short while; our first attraction on this side of the river is the Mirabell Gardens, to your left. After visiting the gardens, we'll shuffle past Mozart's Wohnhaus on the way to our final destination, the Hotel Stein's penthouse café.

⓮ 👋 Go left, scamper past the quartet of chiseled nudes and into the immensely beautiful **Mirabell Gardens** (free to enter, daily, from 6:00 until sundown — **free Wi-Fi** in gardens, "Salzburg surft," click "Einverstanden" to access). Mirabell is the city's most prominent gardens, exhibiting a symphony of color, brilliant reds and yellows and violets, like a painting with tourists. No trip to Salzburg would be complete without a stroll through this fragrant reserve. Fans of the movie "The Sound of Music" particularly love Mirabell because the von Trapp children, plus one governess, donned specially tailored play clothes and frolicked through the gardens singing "Do-Re-Mi" (for more **SOM** highlights in the gardens, see page 92).

Mirabell Palace (in front of you) at the back of the gardens came first in 1606, when Prince-Archbishop Wolf Dietrich von Raitenau built it for his mistress, Salome Alt, who bore him 15 children. At that time the palace was aptly named Altenau and located outside the medieval city. Although the archbishop was truly in love with Salome Alt, their long relationship had to be kept secret on account of his ecclesiastical position as ruler of Salzburg. (In addition to Dietrich's impious behavior, he suffered a number of political and military defeats, which got him deposed in 1612 and subsequently jailed in the fortress as a "prisoner of the pope" until his death in 1617.)

In the 18th century, the immaculate Baroque gardens you see today were landscaped around the palace. After the archbishop surrendered his authority to Napoleon (who in turn surrendered to Austria) in the early 19th century, Emperor Franz Josef officially opened the gardens to the public in 1854 and they've been a cultural magnet to locals and tourists ever since.

Today, Mirabell Palace accommodates the offices of local government like that of the mayor (Bürgermeister) and the marriage registry (Standesamt), as well as a popular venue for classical concerts in the sumptuous Marble Hall, where Mozart himself once played to the delight of the archbishop. The Marble Hall is also where locals are officially obliged by the state to say their wedding vows (before they can hold the ceremony in the church, or location, of their choosing). But Salzburgers aren't complaining because it is recognized as one of the world's most exquisite wedding halls. Wouldn't it be great to say you were married in a palace (with no huge cost involved, only the nominal administrative fee of 150 euros required by the state). If you have a few extra minutes, step into the palace and up to its first floor to see if the doors are open to get a peek at the Marble Hall. (Enter palace via portal adjacent to Pegasus [winged horse] fountain.)

To hear the strains of toe-tapping music outside the palace, hold an ear to the wind for the free hour-long brass-band concerts held openly in the gardens May-August every Wed 20:30 and Sun 10:30.

Lastly, before leaving Mirabell, stand in front of the rose garden, where the graveled path arcs into the grass, and behold a view that is befitting of kings and queens, and you! From this spot (GPS: N47 48.294 E13 02.530), the splendor of the gardens, skyline of the Old Town, and the majesty of the Alps are all at your photographic disposal.

15 Leave the gardens the way you came and carefully cross the road (watching out for cars and buses coming from either direction) straight to **Mozart's Wohnhaus,** (GPS: N47 48.153 E13 02.616, Makartplatz 8, www.mozarteum.at, daily 9:00-17:30 last entry 17:00, July/Aug 8:30-19:00 last entry 18:30, adult 10€, student/senior 8.50€, youth 6-14yr 3.50€  & 15-18yr 4€, family 21€, combo-ticket with Mozart's birthplace available, or free with Salzburg Card, audio guide included with admission, allow 45 min for a visit).

Since Leopold Mozart had made a name for himself as the archbishop's concert meister, in addition to rearing a child prodigy, the Mozarts could afford to move across the river in 1773 to this much bigger, eight-room residence, now a mediocre museum journeying visitors through the family's history and former dominions. Wolfgang lived here until 1780, his sister (Nannerl) until 1784, and Leopold until his death in 1787. Staggeringly, Wolfgang traveled over one-third of his piano-playing life entertaining the various imperial courts of Europe and other dignitaries. Underscoring this feat, near the end of the museum, visitors can synchronize their audio guide with the interactive panel to follow Mozart's numerous concert tours (1762-1791) across the continent totaling some 3,720 days, or more than 10 years and two months on the road; (note that traveling by horse-drawn carriage in those days was not only primitive but grueling and stressful and terribly bumpy, taking what must have seemed like ages to count down the hundreds of miles between destinations, Prague to Paris). Although there are few original furnishings remaining at this residence from the Mozarts' day, Wolfgang's personal Hammerclavier (piano, circa 1781) is fortunately part of the exhibition.

▶ With your back to the Mirabell Gardens, walk the road (Theatergasse) running alongside Mozart's Wohnhaus (weave past the people waiting at the bus stop) towards the main bridge connecting New Town with Old Town (2 min). Stop when you reach the pedestrian plaza opposite the bridge. This is called the Platzl, or "little square." There's usually a crowd of people waiting at the crosswalk for the traffic light to change and on warm days pants-soaked kids playing in the fountains (streams of water) erupting from the ground.

The Hotel Stein is on the corner in front of you but before we venture inside and up to its roof, we're going to first loop around the hotel.

Step into the Platzl, mosey past the fountains, and over to Steingasse on the right. Stop here. We're headed down this cobbled lane but if you were to continue up Platzl, it narrows into shop-lined **Linzergasse**, climbing to the top of New Town. A short way up, on the ground by the Apotheke (**pharmacy**) at Linzergasse 5 (left), is a trio of brass inlaid tablets remembering the Jewish family who once lived here. The Löwy family, Ernst, Ida and son Herbert, were deported in 1942 by the Nazis and murdered at Auschwitz (concentration camp). Farther up, at Linzergasse 41, is St. Sebastian's Cemetery (page 32), where you'd find the **graves of Mozart's father, Leopold and Mozart's widow, Constanze Weber**, as well as the aforementioned Prince-Archbishop Wolf Dietrich von Raitenau.

DIY Old Town Tour

Head down cobbled **Steingasse**. On your left is a pair of petite and atmospheric evening establishments. First up at No. 3, tempting your spicy Latino side, is the **Pepe Cocktail Bar** (page 43) with "tasty cocktails and hot music." Next door, unassuming **Shrimps Bar and Restaurant** (page 49) is a trendy locale specializing in crustacean cuisine, Mediterranean-style (and having outdoor seating in summer). At Steingasse 9 you'll see a *plaque on its facade memorializing the house as the birthplace of **Joseph Mohr** (1792), who penned the world-famous Christmas carol "Silent Night." Adjacent, 256 steps climb to the monastery capping the forested **Kapuzinerberg** (page 38), where a plethora of hiking trails and eye-popping views entice all who make the trip. (*Note: The plaque was incorrectly placed here decades ago; Mohr's correct birthplace is actually Steingasse 31.)

A few meters farther along the lane, as Steingasse narrows, notice the extensive crevices that gouge the right corner wall. These originate from the end of World War II when a U.S. soldier eagerly tried to drive his tank to No. 24 ahead to pick up his hot date. Frustrated, the soldier had to complete his mission on foot, thus he parked his steel beast and marched the short distance to meet his lady in waiting, under the red light at the *Maison de Plaisir*.

Go right here at **Das Kino** (cinema, occasionally screens English-language films), then right at the main road and right again a few doors along into the Hotel Stein. Shuffle straight through the lobby, past reception, up 11 steps, take the elevator to floor 6 and walk up one level to the Stein Terrasse. (Note that **toilets** are located on the 6th floor.)

⑯ ☜ Congratulations! You've reached the **Stein Terrasse** (page 38), the end of our tour. (Sit down, relax, order a beverage. You deserve it.) I hope you enjoyed our walk together and now have a better feel for the City of Mozart, spread before you like the colorful canvas of a Claude Monet painting. If only he ever came here. But you did, thus we celebrate this moment.

I began this tour by saying, "You're fortunate." Look around you; a view of unparalleled beauty extends before your eyes. You're fortunate, and so am I to be able to share this with you. Millions of people around the world can only dream of such a moment, and it's yours to keep, forever.

Before I finish, I want to point out one last site: The red onion steeple you see left of (and beneath) the fortress belongs to the Nonnberg abbey (page 90). Dating from the 8th century, Nonnberg is the first abbey of nuns north of the Alps to follow the Rule of St. Benedict. Together with St. Peter's monastery, the abbey is the epicenter of the Christian community in Salzburg. More recently, Nonnberg starred in the movie, "The Sound of Music." It was an easy choice for Hollywood film scouts. Besides its centuries-old history and architectural splendor, the abbey is where Maria really studied, and where she and the captain really got married. Nonnberg, or Mountain of Nuns, is majestic, solemn and eternal, a place where miracles are said to happen. Perhaps, one has your name on it?

SIGHTS, Old Town

Note: All the attractions listed in this section are either free to enter or are free with the Salzburg Card (page 9), *except* the Glockenspiel tour (page 15).

Fortress (pages 17 & 29), **Mozart's birthplace** (page 22), **DomQuartier** (page 28), **Residenz** (pages 15 & 29), **Festival Halls** (page 20), **Glockenspiel** (page 15), **Cathedral** (page 16), **St. Peter's Cemetery** (page 18), river cruise ("**boat ride**" page 23), **Salzburg Museum** (page 13), **Museums of Modern Art & Natural History** (page 31).

Panorama Museum, www.salzburgmuseum.at, (daily 9:00-17:00, adult 3€, student 1.50€, youth 6-15yr 1€, family 6€, combo-ticket with Salzburg Museum 8.50€/4.50€, or free with Salzburg Card, allow at least 20 min for a visit). **For further details and description of the Panorama Museum,** see page 14.

The main entrance into the Panorama Museum is located off Residenzplatz, behind the cathedral and next to the post office; (you can also enter through the back right of the courtyard leading to the Salzburg Museum). The cashier will give you a leaflet identifying the cosmoramas; (guess the scene by its number on back of leaflet). Behind the cashier are illustrations of the Sattler family and of the original tribute pavilion.

Self-guided panorama: Browse the cosmoramas then enter the panorama (from lower level), climb steps and stand in the middle of the platform with your back to the stairs. Let's say high noon (12:00) on a clock dial is in front of you and the stairway behind you is 6:00. Remember that the panorama is a portrayal of Salzburg as viewed from the fortress in the early 19th century (thus the reason you don't see the fortress). Today, the Old Town is virtually unchanged but the open green fields have largely been converted into housing areas and commercial centers. Note the river was much wilder then. Beer connoisseurs will be happy to know that the church tower at 12:00 (just above white twin towers) represents the monastic Augustinian complex which joins the Müllner Bräu (page 42), Austria's largest tavern and beer garden. At 2:00 (lower part of canvas) is the Dom, or cathedral, where Mozart was baptized in 1756. The twin steeples budding from the distant hill above the Dom (upper part of canvas) belong to the Baroque-style Maria Plain church, a pilgrimage site since the 17th century and today arguably Salzburgland's most magnificent wedding venue. At 5:00 (lower part of canvas) is the Nonnberg abbey—dating from the 8th century, it is the oldest known convent in the German-speaking world. This is the abbey portrayed in the movie "The Sound of Music," and where Maria really studied. At 7:00, the snowcapped Tennengebirge mountains in the background is where you need to be to explore the world's largest ice cave (see Werfen page 66). At 9:00 is Schloss Leopoldskron (palace built in 1736 for the archbishop but more recently recognized as the back of the von Trapp house in "The Sound of Music." Remember the scene the kids fell in the lake?). And it is upon the imposing mountain (Untersberg) rising above the lake that Maria confesses she was singing (in the opening scene of the movie). Use one of the provided telescopes to zoom in on the painting's impressive detail.

DomQuartier, www.domquartier.at, (Wed-Mon 10:00-17:00, closed Tue, last entry 16:00 — July/Aug open daily, Wed till 20:00), price includes audio guide and admission into the Residenz state rooms (and its painting gallery), Museum of St. Peter, the Cathedral Museum (and onto its scenic terrace), and the temporary exhibitions of the North Oratory, adult 12€, student 5€, family 27€, child 5yr or younger free, or free with Salzburg Card—allow 90 min for a visit!

Billed as Salzburg's Tour de Baroque, the DomQuartier gives visitors an intimate look into the former seat of power held by the ruling prince-archbishops. Set within a handful of adjoining sites in the heart of Salzburg, the newly established cultural center totals some 15,000 square meters, 2000 exhibits, and spans 1300 years of history for the price of one admission. From the upper floors, behold terrific views of Old Town lanes, squares and courtyards while touring grand rooms, galleries, and consuming exhibitions.

The DomQuartier can be entered via Residenzplatz or Domplatz. From the inner courtyard, climb the broad staircase to the state rooms (Prunkräume). At the top, notice the Fackelstein used to snuff flaming hand-held torches, or Fackeln, in centuries past.

Visitors to the DomQuartier will first tour the **Residenz,** www.salzburg-burgen.at, dating from 1102, the former state rooms and living quarters of the prince-archbishops (for further details and description of the Residenz, see page 15).

Residenz Gallery, www.residenzgalerie.at, hung with paintings from the 16th to 19th centuries by European masters, including Rubens and Rembrandt.

The **Museum of St. Peter** contains art treasures from the oldest monastery in the German-speaking world.

The **North Oratory** hosts regularly changing exhibitions.

Cathedral Museum: In addition to pious relics dating from the 12th century, you'll see Austria's largest organ (in the Organ Gallery). From here you can peer over the whole of the cathedral's glorious inner sanctum, Salzburg's spiritual center—this breathtaking sight alone is worth your time! Skip to the other side of the Organ Gallery and face the high altar; the organ to its right (pictured), and partially facing you, Mozart regularly played when he was an organist in the archbishop's court. In total, you count five independent organs; Salzburg Cathedral is the only house of God north of the Alps to maintain this many under one roof. And on special occasions when they're all gloriously played in unison, heavenly spirits seemingly lead saints in song and priests in prayer.

Fortress of Salzburg, www.salzburg-burgen.at, (daily: Jan-April & Oct-Dec 9:30-17:00, May-Sept 9:00-19:00, last entry 45 min before listed closing times—price includes round trip on the cable railway and much more, see "admission ticket" below, adult 11.30€, youth 6-14yr 6.50€, family 26€, or free with Salzburg Card—scan card at turnstile to gain fortress admission and ride cable railway). Allow at least two hours for a fortress visit, and know that you'll need to negotiate a few hundred steps along the way. But that hasn't stopped the some 850,000 of us who visit the fortress every year. **For more on the fortress,** see page 17.

There are two ways to reach the fortress: via cable railway (locally Festungsbahn, departing every 5-10 min) or on foot (steep, 20 min, admission is lowered to adult 8€, youth 6-14yr 4.50€, or free with Salzburg Card).

The **admission ticket** (called the FestungsCard) includes all the attractions within the fortress complex. For example, you can wander through a maze of museums (to reach these follow signs posted on the grounds denoting the letter "B" in a blue box) exhibiting artifacts from the days of the Romans, suits of armor and weaponry from the Middle Ages (in the Fortress Museum), medals and uniforms and machine guns from World War I (in the Rainer Regiment Museum).

When arriving by cable railway, exit top station right to the scenic restaurant or jog left to the heart of the fortress and terrific viewing terrace with guard lookouts. Climb 62 steps (steep) to the fortress grounds, go right then swing left and descend to the door ahead on the right with the red letter "A" to join the **fortress orientation tour**—you may have to wait 10 min for it to start.

Before visiting any museums, I recommend you first take the aforesaid 30-min audio-guide tour of the fortress interior to view the torture chamber, explore state rooms formerly belonging to influential archbishops, witness a royal toilet that "flushed" onto

MORE SIGHTS

the peasants below, and to take in the breathtaking panorama of Salzburg and beyond to Bavaria from the lookout tower. The tour concludes in the Golden Hall where classical (e.g. Mozart) concerts are held. While in the hall, pay particular attention to the second marble pillar from the left. Midway up its left side you'll see a cavity where a canon ball struck it during the Peasants' Uprising in the year 1525. No kidding!

☞ **Catacombs** (Katakomben) **self-guided tour,** allow 15 min (daily 10:00-17:00, May-Sept till 18:00, adult 2€, student/youth 6-16yr 1.50€, or free with Salzburg Card), <u>GPS</u>: N47 47.801 E13 02.689.

In the cliffs overlooking St. Peter's Cemetery are the catacombs, dwellings dug out by Christians in the 3rd century A.D. The caverns are still somewhat of a mystery to historians, who will concede that they were used as a hermitage over the past 1,500 years. Perhaps Salzburg's founding father, Bishop Rupert, initially resided here in 696.

The dugouts were originally enclosed within the composite rock until a landslide exposed them in 1669. The man-made facade we see today was added later. You won't find any bones in the catacombs as the name suggests. However, at the entrance are the graves of Mozart's sister, Maria Anna (a.k.a. Nannerl), and Michael Haydn (prominent composer in Salzburg and brother of Joseph Haydn). When viewing the two graves, you're standing on top of an ossuary (oodles of bones), which was positioned here as an "intermediate" depository when no graves in the cemetery were available. The painting at the cross depicts the Virgin Mary, Jonah and Mary Magdalene flanking Jesus above weak souls praying for absolution in a raging fire. Either side of the painting is the Dance of the Dead (1660), portraying victims of plague.

To your left, climb 48 irregular steps to reach the first level, then go right and follow the walkway to St. Gertrude's chapel, dating from the 4th century. The monks from St. Peter's monastery (next door) still periodically use this chapel today, along with the consecrated altar (1862). The column in the center of the room dates from the 17th century and is a remembrance to those who died during the plague. Adjacent are vaulted niches for clergy. In the back of the chapel (through window) is a section hollowed out for those not yet baptized. The fresco above the entrance dates from the 15th century and portrays the martyrdom of St. Thomas Becket (who was the much-adored Archbishop of Canterbury murdered by followers of Henry II, the King of England, in 1170).

Head back outside and climb nine more steps to a petite platform affording dramatic views of the cemetery and Salzburg's soaring collection of church steeples. Inscribed on the bell to your left is the year "1681."

Climb the final 36 lopsided steps via a narrow passage to reach the Maximus chapel. At the top you'll discover an unconsecrated altar (inlaid tablet is absent), a tiny doorway that once led to further dugouts, and an empty grave with a Latin inscription dating from 1530. It reads: "In 477, Odoacer, the king of the peoples Ruthenians, Geppiden, Goths, Magyars and Herulians fought against the church of God and threw Maximus and 50 of his followers off the cliffs to their ghastly deaths. Odoacer's men went on to destroy the entire province of Noricum with fire and swords." (Noricum is roughly the provincial boundaries of today's Salzburgland.)

Mönchsberg Lift, locally Mönchsbergaufzug (daily 8:00-19:00, Wed and July-Aug till 21:00, round trip 3.50€, one way 2.20€, youth 6-14yr 1.80€/1.10€, family 7€/4.40€, or free with Salzburg Card, www.salzburg-ag.at). Don't forget to utilize this option with your Salzburg Card (no need to wait in line, scan card's barcode at turnstile). This elevator, or Aufzug in German, lifts visitors up to the Mönchsberg (Monks' Ridge) observation terrace, one of Salzburg's most scenic vantage points and therefore a choice setting for Maria and the kids to sing "Do-Re-Mi" in "The Sound of Music." Besides a gargantuan view (best in afternoon), you'll have access to clean toilets, the Museum of Modern Art (next entry) and the scenic m32 café/bar/restaurant.

Historically, a single elevator system was excavated from inside the cliff in 1890, whipping beguiled visitors up the 60-meter shaft in a record two minutes. Today, the same trip takes a mere 30 seconds and the three-elevator system transports approximately 1 million persons per year. **To get there,** <u>GPS</u>: N47 48.039 E13 02.356, the lift is located at Gstättengasse 13. To find it, look above the northwest part of the Old Town for a wood-covered shaft leading up the cliff face; walk towards this and follow the cliff farther along to the road Gstättengasse. Or, if you're outside of the Old Town, ride bus 1, 4, 7, 8 or 10 to Mönchsbergaufzug. **Note:** If the weather is nice, take the elevator up and walk the scenic path down (see Mönchsberg Lift & Hiking Trails page 38).

Museum of Modern Art, (Tue-Sun 10:00-18:00, Wed till 20:00, adult 8€, student-senior & youth 6-16yr 6€, combo-ticket with Mönchsberg Lift 10€/7€, or free with Salzburg Card, www.museumdermoderne.at). At a cost of 22€ million in 2004, Salzburg added the Museum der Moderne (MdM) Mönchsberg to its bevy of A-list attractions. Connoisseurs of contemporary visual arts will embrace the juxtaposition of modernity above the Old Town. Boasting 3,000 m² (32,000 ft²) of exhibition floor space on three levels, MdM's easily recognizable white facade with castle-like turret planted atop the Mönchsberg is accessible via the above-listed "Lift." **Note:** Store your daypack/personal items in one of the lockers provided (insert a 1€ coin but you'll get it back upon reopening locker). Every Wednesday (18:00-19:30) and Sunday (14:00-17:30) students pay only 2€ (and 1.70€ rt for the "Lift").

Museum of Natural History, locally Haus der Natur, (daily 9:00-17:00, adult 8€, student and youth 4-15yr 5.50€, family from 20€, or free with Salzburg Card, allow a few hours for a visit—best on a Thursday or Friday, www.hausdernatur.at). This fun and educational museum, founded in 1924, a favorite with children, is Austria's largest science center, having eight levels of exhibits from outer space matter to sea life (excellent aquariums) and dinosaur displays to reptiles in habitat. On the 2nd floor browse the astronomy room for your estimated weight (in kilograms) on the different planets in our solar system; start with Erde (Earth). I weigh, for example, 175 kg on Jupiter; that's 385 lbs! Who knew. After exploring the cosmos, swing through the neighboring reptile zoo and check out crocs and lizards and other cold-blooded creatures. See if you can stare down a poisonous snake. Journey into the human body on the 4th (top) floor; learn how we see, hear, and smell. If nature's call beckons you away from the action, **toilets** are seated on every floor. Next door in the adjoining Science Center, having some 80 interactive stations, kids can ride the (Palfinger) basket crane or run a turbine to produce electricity. But before all that, plan your trip here around the following happenings: **Aquarium**: the octopus, archer fish, and reef shark are fed every Monday & Thursday at 10:15, piranhas too on Thursday. **Science Center**: big and little kids alike are wowed by the "Magic Chemistry Show" and the "Physics Experience" which typically rotate every other Friday at 10:30 in the lab (shows in German, duration 45 min; hopefully one is scheduled during your stay). Round off your museum tour with a visit to its popular

MORE SIGHTS

indoor-outdoor café on the 1st floor (i.e. one level up). **Note:** store your daypack/personal items in a locker downstairs (insert a 1€ coin but you'll get it back upon reopening locker). **To get there**, the museum is located in the northwest part of the Old Town at Museumsplatz 5, between the river and Mönchsberg Lift.

SIGHTS, New Town (across river)

Note: All the attractions listed in this section are either free to enter or are free with the Salzburg Card (page 9): **Mirabell Gardens** (page 25), **Mozart's second residence** (Wohnhaus page 26), **Kapuzinerberg** (page 38).

St. Sebastian's Cemetery & Church, (daily 9:00-16:00, April-Oct till 18:30). Built in late-Gothic style from 1505-1512, St. Sebastian's Church fronts a quaint cemetery landscaped a century later under the reign of Prince-Archbishop Wolf Dietrich von Raitenau. It makes sense that Wolf Dietrich chose this memorial park for his mausoleum, eternally showcasing his holy eminence within a large stately rotunda marking the center of the grounds. Also buried here are **Philippus Paracelsus**, renowned 16th-century alchemist who cured the incurable; **Mozart's father**, Leopold; and **Mozart's widow**, Constanze Weber. For more on the two Mozarts, flip to pages 100-101. **To get there** from the Old Town, <u>GPS</u>: N47 48.259 E13 02.847, cross the river via the Staatsbrücke (main bridge) and climb Linzergasse to No. 60 (right). On your left step through the wrought-iron gate opening into the cemetery. Inside, go straight to Wolf Dietrich and en route you'll pass the Mozarts at the third grave site on the left.

SIGHTS, outside the Old and New towns

Note: All the attractions listed in this section are either free to enter or are free with the Salzburg Card (page 9), *except* for the last two entries: the luge and salt mines.

👍 **Schloss Hellbrunn,** www.hellbrunn.at, (admission and other details at bottom of entry). With its elaborate Baroque gardens, reflecting pools, romantic grottos and trick fountains landscaped on a sprawling 148-acre reserve, Hellbrunn palace was built for the playful and privileged Prince-Archbishop Markus Sittikus (1612-1619), who opportunely succeeded his uncle, Wolf Dietrich von Raitenau, whom Sittikus had imprisoned in the fortress. In select circles, these ornate and expansive digs became known as a Lustschloss, or palace of pleasure, where jovial parties and lavish celebrations were customary. The trick fountains, or Wasserspiele—specially modified statues, footpaths and walls—were a favorite of the archbishop, who giddily lured visitors into the gardens to run a gauntlet of spraying water. The big laugh came when Sittikus invited his guests to the luncheon table, where he seated them onto marble blocks fashioned into stools rigged with concealed water spouts. When Sittikus gave the signal, cold Alpine water shot from the stools—except his, of course—once again saturating his guests, who had to sit unflustered and appreciate that they were the butt of yet another heavenly gag contrived by the archbishop.

A visit to Schloss Hellbrunn is a delightful experience, in particular the trick fountains on a warm summer day. Families will appreciate the open green spaces and playground for kids, not forgetting the Salzburg Zoo (see next entry) and its adorable animals just next door. Fans of the movie "The Sound of Music" will discover the famed gazebo (see Schloss Hellbrunn page 95). Adventurers will trek one hour to the Stein Theater (signs point the way), where on August 31, 1617, the first open-air opera north of the Alps was performed: "L'Orfeo" by Monteverdi. Visitors in December will experience the spirit of Christmas in the palace courtyard, with its decorative market and festivities.

Since Schloss Hellbrunn covers many acres and attractions, a visit here could easily take half a day, depending on your agenda. If you're not carrying the Salzburg Card, I recommend you allow at least 30 min to stroll the gardens (free to enter). Consider a picnic? **Toilets** can be found opposite the gazebo as well as near the palace entrance.

During your visit, you'll notice a canary-yellow structure on the hillside. In 1615, Prince-Archbishop Sittikus required an extra guest house for visiting VIPs, thus he ordered one to be built. The archbishop's labor force completed the task within a month, and from this stellar effort the structure originated its name: Monatsschlössl, or Month Villa. Today, it is the state-run Volkskunde (Folklore) Museum exhibiting items typifying regional cultures and traditions (April-Oct, daily, 10:00-17:30, 2.50€/1.50€, free with Salzburg Card or free with your combo palace-and-fountains ticket).

Stop by the palace March 27 thru Nov 1, 2015, daily (end times denote last tour)—April and Oct (thru Nov 1) 9:00-16:30, May-June and Sept 9:00-17:30, July-Aug 9:00-21:00 (after 18:00 trick fountain tours only), closed Nov-March. The **park and gardens** are free to enter and open daily year round 6:30-17:00, March and Oct till 18:00, April-Sept till 21:00. **Price** (combo-ticket palace and fountains), adult 10.50€, student 7€, youth 4-18yr 5€, family (2+2) 27€, or free with Salzburg Card. **Tours** of the palace interior are at your own pace with an audio guide and take about 25 min (typically no wait time); tours of the trick fountains are led by a palace guide and take roughly 35 min (with wait times upwards of 45 min, depending on weather and crowd size). **Note:** When touring the fountains, if the ground ahead of you is wet, prepare for soakage! On a warm summer's day, however, this is a welcome reprieve (but the line to get in will not be). **To get there**, <u>GPS</u>: N47 45.790 E13 03.847, Schloss Hellbrunn is located 5 km south of the Old Town. **By bus** from the city, hop on #25 direction Untersbergbahn and get off at Hellbrunn, 15-min ride (free with Salzburg Card—bus departs Hauptbahnhof, Mirabellplatz, Rathaus, Mozartsteg every 20 min, and every 30 min after 18:00 Mon-Fri and 17:00 Sat/Sun). **Drivers**, exit the A10 autobahn at Salzburg-Süd and follow signs to Salzburg. At the first traffic light, turn left. On the other side of the village (Anif) you'll see the zoo's natural enclosures (right)—continue past the zoo and turn right at the end of the golden wall. Parking is available in three lots (but I recommend the last one on the right. Take a ticket: first 30 min are free, up to 2hr/2€, 3hr/2.60€, max 3.20€). **Cyclists**, ride pleasant Hellbrunner Allee (via Freisaalweg) to Hellbrunn—(consider riding riverside path back).

Zoo, Salzburg, (daily: 9:00-16:30 last entry 15:30, April-May & Sept-Oct till 18:00 last entry 17:00, June-Aug till 18:30 last entry 17:30, adult 10.50€, youth 4-14yr 4.50€ & 15-19yr 7€, senior 65yr+ 9.50€, family [2+1] 24.50€, or free with Salzburg Card, bag of animal food 3€, allow at least two hours for a visit, www.salzburg-zoo.at). In the early 15th century, the archbishop's love for animals motivated his holiness to establish a wildlife habitat 5 km south of the Old Town. This evolved into today's 35-acre Hellbrunn Zoo (adjacent to the above-listed Schloss Hellbrunn), attracting upwards of 300,000 visitors annually. The zoo is home to around 1,200 animals (representing 140 species), such as zebras, lions, leopards, kangaroos, tigers, wolves, brown bears, rhinos, lemurs and monkeys, to name a few. Several of the enclosures have been landscaped into the cliff face, providing many animals a natural-as-can-be environment. **Note** that Fri and Sat nights from Aug 7 thru Sept 12, 2015 the zoo is open till 22:30 (last entry 21:00), allowing visitors a unique look into the nocturnal world of animals. **To get there**, <u>GPS</u>: N47 45.388

MORE SIGHTS

E13 03.803, follow the same directions above for Schloss Hellbrunn except **by bus** get off at the zoo (one stop after Hellbrunn) and **cyclists** lock the bike up at the palace and stroll through the gardens to the zoo. **Drivers**, exit the A10 autobahn at Salzburg-Süd and follow signs to Salzburg. At the first traffic light, turn left. On the other side of the village (Anif) you'll see the zoo's natural enclosures on the right. Free parking out front (take ticket at boom gate and have zoo cashier validate it).

Brew World, locally Brauwelt, (daily 10:00-17:00, last entry 16:00, July-Aug till 19:00, last entry 18:00, adult 11€, student 10.30€, free with Salzburg Card, allow at least 90 min for a visit, www.brauwelt.at). The folks at Stiegl have been brewing Salzburg's beer since 1492, when Columbus discovered the Americas. To complement Stiegl's 500-year evolution, management put together "Europe's largest brewery exhibition." Tour the interactive museum at your own pace; en route you'll pass the world's biggest (43-liter) beer mug and a 15-foot beer tower (Bierturm) stacked with hundreds of beer bottles representing Austria's bountiful brands and breweries. (Note there are about 100 breweries in Austria.) After your tour, enjoy a couple of freshly brewed Stiegl beers on the house anywhere in the house, e.g. in the saloon, beer garden (courtyard), or you can even redeem your beer coupons in Stiegl's delicious Austrian-style restaurant to complement your meal. **Note:** Your admission ticket is also valid for a free remembrance gift; typically your choice of either a bottle of Stiegl beer or a beer glass. **To get there,** GPS: N47 47.613 E13 01.355, Brauwelt is located at Bräuhausstrasse 9, 2 km west of the Old Town. **By bus** from the city, hop on #1 direction Europark/Red Bull Arena and get off at Bräuhausstrasse, 10-min ride (free with Salzburg Card—bus departs Hauptbahnhof, Mirabellplatz, Makartplatz, Hanuschplatz every 10 min, and every 20 min after 19:00 Mon-Sat and all day Sun). Exit bus left and make the next left on Bräuhausstrasse. The brewery entrance is a few minutes farther ahead on the right. **Drivers**, from the city it's tough to find—ask directions. From the A1 autobahn, exit at "Flughafen" and follow signs to Salzburg/Brauwelt. After driving through the airport underpass, make your second right onto Karolingerstrasse. Follow this straight to the T-intersection at the end, where you'll turn left. Go straight, the road will curve right, and follow Brauwelt signs closely for the upcoming right turns that circle the brewery and lead into the free visitor parking lot.

Hangar-7, (daily 9:00-22:00, free entry, www.hangar-7.com). Head over to the airport and into Hangar-7, an ultramodern shelter made of glass and steel to house a collection of vintage aircraft dubbed the Flying Bulls. Upon arriving, you'll be greeted with a boarding pass permitting you access to the hangar to get acquainted with some modern jets and a few of history's legendary aircraft, such as the B-25 Mitchell bomber (pictured), F4U Corsair, Lockhead P-38 Lightning, and a DC-6 (that was formerly Yugosla-

via's Air Force One equivalent used to transport Marshal Tito and his centrist guests). From the display floor, look up. Integrated into the apex of the hangar's ceiling is the translucent **Threesixty Bar** (closed Mon & Thur otherwise open from 18:30), featuring a glass floor giving patrons the feel of walking on air. Hangar-7—sponsored by Red Bull (page 70), the energy drink—was inaugurated on August 22, 2003 before a crowd of 10,000, including Prince Albert of Monaco, U.S. astronaut "Buzz" Aldrin, and F1 race-car champion Niki Lauda. The event raised nearly $2 million for charity.

Other reasons to visit Hangar-7 are its first-rate bar-lounges and restaurant, revolving art exhibitions, and arguably the poshest restroom you'll see in Salzburg (downstairs). At the fine **Ikarus** restaurant (daily 12:00-14:00 & 19:00-22:00, reservations recommended, tel. 0662/21970, e-mail: ikarus@hangar-7.com) not only does the menu change monthly but so does the cook! Each year 12 of the world's best chefs are invited here for the month to prepare their signature dishes alongside those of their native country. Also dissimilar to other restaurants, pilots can literally fly in and park their plane out front. Salzburg's first non-smoking bar, **Mayday** (daily 12:00-midnight, Fri/Sat till 01:00) serves a wide range of hand-shaken drinks and healthy, "smart" cuisine. **Carpe Diem** café-lounge (daily 9:00-17:00, breakfast Mon-Fri 9:00-11:30 and Sat/Sun till 14:00) is a modish place to gel and consume beverages and snacks flown in from around the world while sitting only meters from a World War II fighter-bomber. **To get there**, GPS: N47 47.624 E13 00.498, Hangar-7 is located on the east side of the airport at Wilhelm-Spazier-Strasse 7. **By bus** from the city, hop on #2 direction Airport/Walserfeld and get off at Karolingerstrasse, 20-min ride (free with Salzburg Card—bus departs Wolf-Dietrich-Str., Mirabellplatz, Hauptbahnhof every 10 min, and every 20 min after 19:00 Mon-Sat and all day Sun). From Karolingerstrasse, it's a 5-min walk, exit bus left and march to the forward traffic light. Cross the street, continue straight (on Wilhelm-Spazier-Strasse) and Hangar-7 is a few hundred meters farther ahead on the right. **Drivers**, free parking. When coming from the city, turn left before the airport underpass into Wilhelm-Spazier-Strasse. When coming from the A1 autobahn, exit at "Flughafen" and follow signs to Salzburg. After driving through the airport underpass, make the first right into Wilhelm-Spazier-Strasse.

Untersberg Mountain & Cable Car,
(cable cars run daily every 30 min on the hour and half hour from 9:00-16:00, March-June & Oct 8:30-17:00, July-Sept 8:30-17:30—but note the system will be closed for maintenance April 13-24 & Nov 9 thru Dec 11, 2015—round trip adult 22€, student 15€, youth 6-14yr 11€, dog 7.50€, or free with Salzburg Card, www.untersbergbahn.at; allow 90 min for a visit, not counting travel time to/fro cable car). Arguably Austria's most captivating landmass, Untersberg is a moun-

tain of myth and legend spawned by medieval tales immortalizing heroic emperors and fantastic creatures that dwell in its foothills, peaks and valleys. In more recent times, Hollywood discovered Untersberg's charm and portrayed a dirndl-clad girl singing "The Sound of Music" on its meadows that led her to the abbey (page 90). Midway along Untersberg's extensive plateau, a V-shaped crevice forms the natural border between Germany (Bavaria) and Austria. A short distance away at Ober-

salzberg, Hitler used to stare past Untersberg's majestic mass and into Salzburg from his giant picture-frame window (at his home, the Berghof). From its valuable marble quarries (still in operation today), Untersberg has been a premier source of building material over the centuries for the construction of numerous structures and statues in the Salzburg region and as far away as Hungary.

But most important, the mountain is home to a sensational **cable car system** (called the Untersbergbahn, built 1959-61) that was used in the filming of the 1968 movie, "Where Eagles Dare" with Clint Eastwood and Richard Burton. If you get a chance, throw your travels into high gear and ride the cable car up to the scenic heights of Untersberg (pictured here towering above Salzburg's Old Town). The mountain peaks at 1,865 m (6,117 ft), but the cable car docks at 1,776 m (5,825 ft). This is a perch from which God sits, and from where you can see the world—but more directly the Eagle's Nest, the

Watzmann (Germany's second-largest mountain), the inviting lakes of the Salzkammer-gut, and the glacier ice of the Hohe Tauern. You can enjoy these sights with a hot cup of Glühwein (mulled wine) if you arrive before the snow melts (typically by the end of April). The 50-person cabin will climb the mountain and reach the summit within 9 breathtaking minutes. (Simultaneously, a second cabin will descend from the mountain.) You'll notice that only two pylons support the whole system, which can be a petrifying thought to some people. Thus, with the price of your ticket, you may receive an extra pair of underwear! **To get there**, the Untersberg cable car station is located 13 km south of Salzburg's Old Town. **By bus** from the city, hop on #25 direction Untersbergbahn and ride it to the end, 30 min (free with Salzburg Card—bus departs Hauptbahnhof, Mirabell-platz, Rathaus, Mozartsteg every 20 min, and every 30 min after 18:00 Mon-Fri and 17:00 Sat/Sun). **Drivers**, exit A10 autobahn at Salzburg-Süd and head direction Grödig—after 1 km you'll see the cable car station on the right (turn at traffic light).

Casino, (free entry but must be at least 18 years of age to enter, ID required; open 364 days, 15:00-03:00, slots from 12:00, closed Dec 24, tel. 0662/854-4550, CC: VC, MC, DC; www.casinos. at). Gamblers, try your luck in Salzburg's mag-nificent Baroque casino, set in an 18th-century  palace: Schloss Kleßheim, once home to Prince-Archbishop Firmian. (Converted into a casino in 1934 but closed during the war and reopened in 1950.) A handful of poker, roulette and black jack tables, along with 150 slot machines (called Automaten) await your providential touch. Men are required to wear a jacket and an appropriate shirt (or the casino can typically loan what you need for a nominal fee). No tennis or sports shoes permitted. Ladies, there's no real dress code for you, just look like a winner. Although admission is free, registration is mandatory and a photo ID required. **To get there**, GPS: N47 49.098 E12 59.761, Schloss Kleßheim is located 4 km northwest of the Old Town. **By Casino Shuttle:** The shuttle (available from 16:30) can pick you up in town or drop you off after; have staff at your hotel arrange the transfer or tel. 0662/222-0777. **By bus** from the city, every second bus 1 stops in front of the casino (direction Red Bull Arena—con-firm casino stop with driver), 25-min ride (free with Salzburg Card—bus departs Haupt-bahnhof, Mirabellplatz, Hanuschplatz every 20 min until about 22:00). **Drivers**, exit A1 autobahn at Kleßheim, parking is free in front of palace.

Luge Ride, Dürrnberg, (in good weather May 1 thru Oct 18, 2015, daily 11:00-17:00, mid-June thru mid-Sept 10:00-18:00, tel. 06245/85105, www.duerrnberg.at, adult one ride 9.30€, two/16.30€, three/21.50€, 20% off with valid Salzburg Card, stu-dents and families receive discount, combo-ticket with Dürrnberg salt mines 24.30€). Located some 20 km south of Salzburg, above the town of Hallein at Dürrnberg (near salt mines, see next entry), is the mother of all Austrian toboggan runs at 2.2 km (1.4 mi) long! Forget all those other so-called toboggan runs, locally Sommerrodelbahn, this exhilarating and wildly scenic luge ride will make the hair on the back of your neck stand at attention. No kidding! The course is idyllically set upon the peak of a mountain, thus a lengthy yet enjoyable chair lift will carry you to the summit, where the flora is lush and the views are sensational! What's more, a short hike from the top station will land you on the German border. When you're ready to ride the luge down, head to the departure area and the operator will supply your sled. Beware, this is not for the faint hearted—it is steep (57% grade), the corners are sharp, and the track is swift! If you want to go full-throttle, allow at least a few minutes to pass before beginning your run so as not to catch the slowpokes ahead of you. Trust me, if one person before you in the previous 5 minutes throttles at a Sunday pace, your speed record is toast! Before you ride down, relax at the summit, explore nature, snap memorable photos, have a beverage at the chalet (or, better yet, throw down a picnic). GPS: N47 39.592 E13 05.558, Weissenwäschweg 19, Bad Dürrnberg. **Railers** (from Salzburg to the luge is roughly a 50-min journey—Salzburg Card *not* valid—www.svv-info.at), outside Hallein train station hop on bus 41 to Zinkenlift (bus departs every hour typically :55 min past the hour). From the Zinkenlift stop to the luge cashier is a short stroll through a quaint neighborhood. **Drivers**, exit A10 autobahn at Hallein (No. 16) and follow brown signs to Salzwelten (meaning salt mines, which are also denoted by a pick-and-hammer symbol). On the other side of town the road will climb to Dürrnberg; after 3 km the salt mines will appear on the right. (To reach the toboggan:) Continue another kilometer farther to the chair lift and parking area on the left. The cashier is a short stroll through a quaint neighborhood. **But if you're driving** from Berchtesgaden, ask TI (or a local) for directions because the luge and salt mines are less than 10 km via spectacularly scenic country roads.

Salt mines, which one is best? Some travelers may be wondering which salt mine is best to visit, Berchtesgaden or Dürrnberg? By far the busier mine is Berchtesgaden (see my "Berchtesgaden & Hitler's Eagle's Nest" guide) because it's cheaper and practically on the way to the Eagle's Nest. However, unlike Berchtesgaden, the Dürrnberg mine offers dynamite views and a reconstructed Celtic village to explore. As for the mines themselves, both are virtually the same: offering deep caverns, wooden slides, and a salty lake. So, to answer the question, which mine is better: they both are (but if I *had* to pick one, it'd be Dürrnberg). Bottom line: Visit whichever mine best suits your travel itinerary, this includes the world's oldest mine in Hallstatt (page 78), which is also excellent.

Salt Mines, Dürrnberg, (April-Oct tours depart regularly every day from 9:00 until last tour at 17:00, and Nov-March hourly 10:00-15:00, except closed for routine maintenance Oct 22-23 2015 & Jan 11-29, 2016, www.salzwelten.at, adult 19€ [with valid Salzburg Card 15.20€], student/senior 17€, family [2+1/2+2/1+1] 40€/48.50€/25€; allow two hours for a visit, not counting travel time to/fro mines—note that tours roughly run 75 min). Some 2,500 years ago, Celtic peoples migrated to Dürrnberg (mountain above town of Hallein, about 20 km south of Salzburg) to quarry salt. The Celts found tons of the "white gold" here, thus many communities in the region begin or end with the Celtic word Hall, meaning salt. From this ancient settlement above Hallein developed a prosperous salt mine, featuring a subterranean labyrinth of deep tunnels, crystal galleries, swooshing slides and a salty lake. For more than a millennium, "white gold" filled the coffers of Salzburg's archbishops, as well as the Habsburgs who chronologically followed. Today, salt mining on Dürrnberg has gone the way of the dodo bird and the only mining still in operation is the extraction of money from tourists, who throw on white overalls and experience the former salt caverns like a themed ride at Disneyland. Outside, visitors are treated to a reconstructed Celtic village and distant views of Salzburg. **Note:** Combine a visit to the salt mines with a sprint down Austria's longest luge (see previous entry). GPS: N47 40.017 E13 05.460, Ramsaustrasse 3, Bad Dürrnberg. **Railers** (from Salzburg to the mines is roughly a 50-min journey—Salzburg Card *not* valid—www. svv-info.at), outside Hallein train station hop on bus 41 to Salzbergwerk (bus departs every hour typically :55 min past the hour). **Drivers**, see directions for Drivers in the previous entry for Luge Ride.

For more sites and attractions outside of Salzburg, see Excursions on page 64.

MORE SIGHTS

BEST VIEWS & HIKES

Stein Terrasse, (daily 7:00-midnight, Fri-Sat till 01:00, breakfast 7:00-11:00, tel. 0662/874-346-700, **free Wi-Fi**). Atop the Hotel Stein is the must-visit Stein Terrasse, meaning "stone terrace," a rooftop café featuring astonishing views of Salzburg Old Town crowned by its medieval fortress, making hotshots out of novice photographers. I'd argue this is the most impressive café view in all of Austria! Grab a table, order a beverage, relax, enjoy! (Note, the café can be *very* busy at times, in which case the service may be slow.) **To get there,** Hotel Stein can be found at Giselakai 3, adjacent to the river (right bank) and main bridge (Staatsbrücke) crossing to/fro the Old Town. Skip straight through the lobby, past reception, up 11 steps, take the elevator to floor 6 and walk up one level to the Stein Terrasse. **Toilets** located on the 6th floor.

Fortress, locally Festung Hohensalzburg, (page 17). From the turrets of Salzburg's millennium-old fortress are fabulous views of the Old Town and beyond.

Müllnersteg: Exceptional view of the Old Town can be captured from the Müllnersteg pedestrian bridge (best results in the afternoon).

Untersberg Mountain & Cable Car, (page 35). If you have the time, especially if you're holding a Salzburg Card, this elevating adventure is not to be missed!

Kapuzinerberg & Hiking Trails: Wander up to the yellowed monastery capping the Kapuzinerberg (Capuchins' Ridge on right bank of river) to reach an abundance of trails and stunning views. The monastery can be accessed via two passageways: Linzergasse 14 and also at Steingasse 9. The latter is best. At Steingasse 9 (GPS: N47 48.098 E13 02.767) you'll see a plaque memorializing the birthplace of Joseph Mohr (1792), who penned the world-famous Christmas carol, "Silent Night." From here, climb 256 steps past the adorable St. Johannes chapel (dating from 1319) to the top (steep, 5 min). At the top (of the main grouping of steps) stop, you're only meters away from two lookout points: one is over your right shoulder, and the other is ahead of you (via the three sets of four steps leading to the monastery). For the better view, climb the 11 steps to your right and go right again. At the bottom of the short path you'll happen upon a battle-worthy turret from medieval times, tremendously scenic views of the Old Town, and the beginning of an adventurous hike (left and down). **Note:** If you decide to go for a lengthy hike here, at times you'll feel lost. Just remember, all paths heading west eventually arrive back at the monastery and the other lookout point. However, if you prefer to absorb wowing views to battling bushes, turn around and head straight to the other lookout. Adjacent to it is the monastery, and the descending road comes out at Linzergasse 14. From there, left drops to the river and Old Town, and right climbs to the top of New Town and St. Sebastian's Cemetery (page 32).

Mönchsberg Lift & Hiking Trails: Whiz up the elevator to the Mönchsberg (Monks' Ridge) observation terrace for an unforgettable view of Salzburg (for prices and times see Mönchsberg Lift page 31). If you're keen for a light nature stroll, follow the **self-guided tour**:

From the observation terrace (Aussichtsterrasse), climb the 15 steps and continue straight past the telescope onto the graveled trail. Parallel the iron railing a short distance (railing will change to wood)—don't follow the trail leading down—veer right (on trail forking right) and pass the wooden shack on your left. Fortifications will appear on your left and soon the trail will connect onto a paved (asphalt) route. Follow paved route through the arched passage ahead (and with a little imagination, you've stepped through a time warp to the Middle Ages). At the top, swing left to the plaque (against stone wall right of archway). It reads: "Here the citizens built a defense system consisting of four towers and a wall, as this is the narrowest part of the Mönchsberg. In 1488, citizen watch units were first referred to as the Salzburg Guard, and in 1816 they were dissolved." Now, over your right shoulder, wander to the benches and check out the terrific view—that's Bavaria in the distance (pointy mountain); below it is Salzburg Airport. When ready, walk the trail behind you running alongside the old fortified wall. At the end you'll reach a spectacular lookout over Salzburg. On the way back step through the narrow portal (left) to the café-restaurant Stadtalm (page 51). Beyond the cafe, follow the (paved) path as it swings left and up to the fork—go straight to the **fortress** (Festung, 15 min) or left and down to the **Old Town** (Altstadt). The 330 steps descending to town are called the Clemens Holzmeister Stiege, named after the famous Austrian architect who designed the festival halls (page 21) located at the bottom.

Mozart Balls

Salzburg is a city of chocolate balls. Boxes upon boxes, in all shapes and sizes, filled with little sweets wrapped in shiny foil. People travel to Salzburg from all over Europe for a taste of an authentic Mozartkugel, or Mozart ball, made of chocolate, nougat, marzipan, pistachio, and more chocolate. Yum. There are actually three different companies that produce Mozart balls. The original balls, however, come from Café Fürst (page 49), established in 1884 by Paul Fürst. Paul created his first ball in 1890 and he soon began winning international awards. It wasn't long before other confectioners copied his idea. Even though Paul's balls were  first, you won't regularly see them around town. The Fürst family believes in quality, not quantity, as a statement by Paul Fürst explains: "I am of the basic opinion that the Mozartkugel is a sweet, and not a Mozart souvenir to be sold at unsuitably sunlit street stands." Paul's Mozart balls are still made from the original recipe and are recognizable by their blue-and-silver foil wrapping. Try one, 1€.

SHOPPING

In need of some retail therapy? Check out Salzburg's contemporary shopping mall at Europark or window shop medieval lanes in the Old Town. And then there's a store that sells only eggs, lots of 'em! But first, I want to point out…

Something Traditional: For an authentic (albeit pricey) gift from Salzburg, like lederhosen or hand-knitted socks, first head over to Salzburger Heimatwerk on Residenzplatz then cross the square to Jahn-Markl. Browse **Salzburger Heimatwerk** (Mon-Fri 9:00-18:00, Sat 9:00-17:00, all major CCs accepted, www.sbg.heimatwerk.at, tel. 0662/844-110) to get in touch with authentic Austrian fabrics, handicrafts, dressmaking materials, silks, alpine designs, and traditional Salzburger costume (called Tracht) like lederhosen and dirndls. But don't limit yourself to Heimatwerk, also browse the much smaller but much older **Jahn-Markl** store, Salzburg's most venerated dressmaker, since 1408, (Mon-Fri 9:30-18:00, Sat 9:30-15:00, tel. 0662/842-610, www.jahn-markl.at, located in the right corner of Residenzplatz, a couple of doors before Alter Markt, or Old Market Square). Jahn-Markl is pricey, but it's the real deal. Inside its narrow doorway is a room resplendent with lederhosen, dirndls, suspenders, belts, hats, deerskin jackets and slippers, hand-knitted socks and hand-stitched gloves, all handmade locally. They also repair leather garments.

👆 **Sporer Wines & Spirits,** (Mon-Fri 9:30-19:00, Sat 8:30-17:00, tel. 0662/845-431, Getreidegasse 39, www.sporer.at). This long-established business goes hand-in-glove with the above theme of "traditional" Salzburg.

Franz Sporer founded this petite yet atmospheric wine-and-spirits shop and tavern here at Getreidegasse 39 way back in 1903, but the building itself, the narrowest in the lane, was first mentioned 500 years earlier in 1407. Now a fourth-generation family run business, Sporer specializes in an intoxicating selection of Austrian wines and schnapps and brandy, but for Salzburgers Sporer has long been considered a Geheimtip, or "secret" tip, on account of its home-distilled liqueur (e.g. cherry, walnut, peppermint, apricot, cinnamon) and punch (orange, Christmas) that are arguably just as medicinal, or capable of combating ill health, as alcoholic. Many of the "house" blends are stored in 100-year-old wooden casks propped against the stone wall opposite the service counter. Customers readily return with their bottle in hand to refill at a reduced price. The most popular Sporer blend is its orange punch (50% abv, 15.40€ half liter), first concocted by (grandfather) Otto in 1927 using an agreeable mix of oranges, lemons, liqueurs, rum and a few secret ingredients. When I say the latter orange punch is popular, I'm hardly exaggerating, many Salzburgers keep a bottle of it in their pantry or medicine cabinet. And a friend of mine in town politely told me not to let this Geheimtip out of the bag. But she's just gonna have to forgive my desire to fill you in. So stop by Sporer's small but pleasant non-smoking shop and tavern when you have time and taste test a few local secrets while mingling with a few locals. **Note:** A bottle of punch is a thoughtful gift idea. Staff speak English and will be pleased to help you choose your tonic. While there, try a shot of punch (orange, Christmas) or liqueur, but it's cheaper to imbibe by the glass. **Drivers,** if you parked in the Altstadt Garage (page 8), have the Sporer cashier validate your ticket so you only pay 4€/4hr or 6€/8hr to park.

👆 **Getreidegasse,** meaning "grain lane," is Salzburg's historic shopping street, an adoring pedestrian thoroughfare chock-full of tourists and locals alike scampering beneath an eclectic array of gilded wrought-iron signs hanging over retail stores. Because many people were illiterate in medieval times, signs like these were commonplace, symbolizing the trade performed at each place of business; for example, a loaf of bread meant a bakery, or a shoe suggested a cobbler (footwear specialist), or a big golden M indicated hot fries and burgers. Getreidegasse gets really congested around the rich-yellow facade at No. 9, Mozart's birthplace (Geburtshaus). At its western end, Getreidegasse opens into the Old Market Square (page 21) then Judengasse before flowing into Mozartplatz where you'll find the TI, among other sites.

Easter-Egg Shop, (open year round, 365 days, Mon-Sat 9:00-19:00, Sun 9:00-18:00, from 3.90€/egg, CC: VC, MC). Yes, those are decorated eggs you saw in the window. Back up, walk by again, but you'll see the same thing: Easter eggs (and most all are hand painted by artists who reside in Austria, thus each is unique). Trays stacked upon trays of the colorful hard-shelled objects fill the shop. And not just chicken eggs, there are quail eggs and turkey eggs and ostrich eggs, too. The owner told me she has upwards of 500,000 eggs, but not just for Easter, also Christmas and Halloween! You've gotta see this place for yourself. Really! Pick up an egg carton and browse around. **To get there,** the shop is located at Judengasse 9. If you're standing in front of and facing Mozart's birthplace at Getreidegasse 9, go left and continue straight. After the Old Market Square (Alter Markt) the lane becomes Judengasse and the egg shop is ahead on the left. Or, when facing the Mozartplatz TI, jog left then right around the corner and down into Judengasse; the shop will soon appear on the right.

Judengasse: You'll discover antique and specialty shops on this Jewish Lane as well as the quaint lanes running off it. While here, pop into the above-listed Easter-egg shop—use its directions to find this part of the Old Town.

Europark, (www.europark.at, Mon-Thur 9:00-19:30, Fri 9:00-21:00, Sat 9:00-18:00). This Olympic-sized shopping mall is the pride of retail Austria and a cash cow for Salzburg. If you're ever wondering where all the locals are, come here. Europark is home to more than 130 eateries and shops, including Ikea, Lacoste, Puma, Zara, Esprit, Levi's, H&M fashion, and an enormous Inter Spar supermarket. **To get there,** GPS: N47 48.922 E13 00.534, Europark is located at Europastrasse 1, 3 km northwest of the Old Town. **By bus,** ride #1 to Europark (which departs from the city at Hauptbahnhof, Mirabellplatz, Hanuschplatz every 10 min, direction Europark/Red Bull Arena, 25-min ride); buses 20 and 28 also depart regularly from Hanuschplatz. **Drivers,** from the A1 autobahn, exit at "Kleßheim." Parking is free and won't be a problem since there are literally thousands of spaces available, many of which are in one of Europe's largest combined underground garages.

Outlet Center, (www.designer-outlet-salzburg.at, Mon-Thur 9:30-19:00, Fri 9:30-19:00, Sat 9:00-18:00). Although this newish designer outlet center (opened Sept 2009) is a novel concept for Salzburg, I found that even with discounts of 30-70% the merchandise still to be costly (with much of the apparel seemingly priced in the hundreds of euros). One thing for sure, I'm no clever fashion shopper; perhaps you will find a bargain. There are some 100 retail outlets in the outlet center featuring name brands such as Calvin Klein (Jeans), Oakley, Escada, Valentino, Hugo Boss, Columbia. **To get there,** the indoor Outlet center is situated at Kasernenstrasse 1, Wals-Himmelreich, right off the A1 autobahn by Salzburg airport 5 km west of the Old Town. **Drivers,** exit the A1 autobahn at "Flughafen"; park free the first two hours then 2€/hr thereafter (but waived if you spend 150€+ shopping—show receipt to Center Info desk). **By bus** from the city, hop on #2 direction Airport/Walserfeld and get off at Designer Outlet (DOC), 20-min ride (bus departs Wolf-Dietrich-Str., Mirabellplatz, Hauptbahnhof every 10 min, and every 20 min after 19:00 Mon-Sat and all day Sun); bus 10 also departs regularly from Hanuschplatz.

ENTERTAINMENT

Another Salzburg plus is its welcomed absence of in-your-face neon signs promoting the latest bar, pachinko parlor or kitschy café. Maintaining age-old tradition, this type of advertising is strictly *verboten*. With a little patience you'll discover a wealth of nightlife behind inconspicuous, 19th-century facades—especially along the riverside. **Note:** Famished night owls consider heavenly Troja kebabs (page 48) before hitting the hay.

Those of you who enjoy drinking a beer with history on your side, take note of the following three establishments: Müllner Bräu, Stieglkeller, and Die Weisse.

👆 **Müllner Bräu,** dating from 1621, is Austria's largest tavern and beer garden (www.augustinerbier.at, daily 15:00-23:00, weekends from 14:30, liter of Augustiner beer 6€, 3€ half liter, <u>cash only</u>!). A venerable complex of beer halls adjoined by a leafy 1,500-seat beer garden, Müllner Bräu is not surprisingly situated in the district of "Mülln," named after the umpteen mills that once populated the landscape. In 1605, Augustinian Hermits settled the area, becoming a frothy monastic district of prayer and beer making. Since the 19th century, dry-mouthed citizens have been pouring into Mülln for the Augustinian specialty: beer. At the on-site brewery, the monks still insist that their beer is stored in wooden

kegs, giving it an all-natural taste intoxicatingly popular with locals and beer buffs. Inside Müllner Bräu, a row of food counters dish up Austrian fare (although I'm not overly keen for this oft greasy spoon) and old-world beer halls feature coffee-colored wood paneling, stained-glass windows, and Gothic typeface drafted upon *smoke-stained walls. (*Note that Saal [hall] "1" is now non-smoking.) Outside, heady locals bask under a forest of chestnut trees (Kastanienbäume) quaffing liter-sized brews in Austria's largest beer garden. **Note:** Pay for your beer at the cashier, pick out your clay mug, give it a rinse, head to the Schenke (place where beer is served) and hand your receipt to the Kegmeister along with your empty mug. To complement your brew, choose some grub from the afore-said food counters inside or you are allowed to bring in your own picnic items (but drinks must be purchased here). When leaving Müllner Bräu, stop by the nearby pedestrian bridge (Müllnersteg) for a phenomenal view of the Old Town. **To get there** (Müllner Bräu), <u>GPS</u>: N47 48.336 E13 01.978, **by bus** from Hanuschplatz (catch bus on river side heading north), ride either 7, 8, 20, 21, 27 (also departs from main train station direction Airport), or 28 a couple of stops to LKH/St.-Johanns-Spital. **By foot** from the Old Town, follow the river (north), pass the boat dock and parallel the Mönchsberg cliffs. Continue straight and the cliff face will taper to a soaring copper-domed church steeple; next door is your oasis. **Drivers**, park in their lot (free) at Lindhofstrasse 7—take ticket at gate and have beer cashier validate it. <u>Note</u>: If you're day parking and wish to reach the Old Town, either follow the river (south) on foot (20 min) or buses regularly pick up from here (ask driver if he's going to Zentrum/Hanusch Platz). Upon return, crown your day with a mug of Salzburg's best beer (have beer cashier validate your park ticket).

The **Stieglkeller** (page 46) is another longstanding institution in Salzburg wor-thy of your time, situated above the Old Town rooftops and below the fortress.

Weissebier fans will cherish **Die Weisse** (Mon-Sat 10:00-midnight, Sudwerk 17:00-02:00), Salzburg's 115-year-old wheat beer microbrewery (since 1901) having an atmospheric tavern, beer garden, and nightspot called **Sudwerk**. Die Weisse's two house specialties are its on-tap "hell" and bottled "dunkel," or light and dark wheat beers, both 5.2% abv. Complementing their award-winning brew, Die Weisse also serves tradition-al Austrian grub (dinner reservations recommended, tel. 0662/872-246). Courting Die Weisse's serious patrons, the brew master kicks it up a notch with its potent seasonal batches and the all-year Jubilator, an extra-strong (8% abv) *doppelbock!* **To get there**, Die Weisse is located at Rupertgasse 10, corner of Bayerhamerstrasse, at the top of New Town via Linzergasse, within a 15-min walk of the Old Town.

For an alcoholic slice of the Emerald Isle, pub and clubgoers begin your evening in the Old Town at No. 12 Rudolfskai (one-way road running along left riverbank) at either Guinness-inspired tavern: **Shamrock** (Mon-Wed 12:00 noon till 03:00, Thur-Sat till

04:00, Sun till 02:00, www.shamrocksalzburg.com) is a fundamental component of Salzburg nightlife with **live music** every evening and clouds of cigarette smoke. Or for less commotion and a separate smoking area, try **O'Malley's** next door (daily, 20:00 till late). Both pubs neighbor each other behind old stone facades and serve a pint of Guinness for around 4.90€. To me Irish mates, *sláinte!* **Note:** Depending on where you're coming from, the easiest way to reach either pub is via Shamrock's back door at Judengasse 1, just off Alter Markt, or Old Market Square.

Continue the fun at **Pepe Cocktail Bar** (Steingasse 3, behind Hotel Stein, Tue-Sat 19:00-03:00), a small joint that hooks its guests on an intoxicating menu of Latin American and Caribbean concoctions consisting of margaritas and daiquiris (pineapple, peach, banana, strawberry, mango), gins, whiskeys, vodkas, rums, tequilas, exotic cocktails and piña coladas, Corona beer, red and white wine, nachos with cheddar cheese and jalapeños. Wednesdays at Pepe's means Havana party night, sip mojitos (5.50€ ea.), dance the conga and smoke Cubans (buy at tobacco vendor en route). Or join the weeklong happy hour Tue-Sat 19:00-21:00 when all cocktails are 5.50€ (usually 6.60€-7.50€).

☞ St. Peter's Stiftskeller (page 46, adjacent to St. Peter's church and cemetery) hosts the delightful and recommended **Mozart-Dinner-Concert** (duration 2.5 hours, concert and 3-course dinner, drinks not included, adult 56€, student 42€, youth 6-14yr 34€, *exclusive package 93€/person [*preferred seating, extended gourmet menu, welcome drink, program booklet], doors open from 19:00 May-Sept [from 18:00 Oct-April], dress smart-casual, CC: VC, MC). Show starts at 20:00 May thru Sept (19:00 rest of year) in the Stiftskeller's historic Baroque hall (upstairs); the best of Mozart is performed by the "Amadeus Consort Salzburg" in period dress. During intermissions, wait staff stride between candlelit tables delivering a multicourse dinner (typically cream soup, chicken breast with vegetables, and dessert) prepared according to recipes from the 18th century. **Tickets** can be purchased at the TI, by phone (0662/828-695), online (www.salzburg-concerts.com), or last minute at the door but at this late hour you risk the show being sold out (particularly May/June Sept & Dec). **Note:** Book the Mozart dinner with your Salzburg Card and get the Mozart concert CD absolutely *free* (confirmed by the full-page ad in your Salzburg Card & Sights brochure). Lastly, drinks are pricey and *not* included in the dinner-show price, thus whatever your bill, a tip (e.g. 10%) would be appreciated by your waiter but it is not expected.

"The Sound of Salzburg Dinner Show" (www.soundofsalzburgshow. com, mid-May thru October almost daily, few performances rest of year) performed live entirely in English by the "Salzburg Sound of Music Singers" is a pleasurable, albeit kitschy, proposition at the Sternbräu restaurant (Griesgasse 23) in the Old Town, doors open 19:00, dinner 19:30, show begin 20:30, show end 22:00, 3-course dinner plus show 54€, youth 7-14yr 34€, or show only [without dinner] plus one drink 34€/18€, free admission for children 6yr and under, book at the door with your Salzburg Card—pay cash—and receive a 5€-11€ discount. Note: CC payment incurs 1€ charge per ticket.

I enjoyed watching the "Salzburg Sound of Music Singers" (two guys and two gals clad in traditional costume) perform the show, a series of entertaining song-and-dance routines set to the best of the movie soundtrack as well as classical and folk hits played by a live pianist. That said, if you're pained by SOM overkill, give this show a miss. If you're keen for more SOM, however, by all means join in the toe-tappin' fun. Heck, you may even get plucked from the audience to sing a chorus with the cast.

Classical concerts sound year round in Salzburg and are a dream in the sumptuous Marble Hall of the Mirabell Palace (www.salzburger-schlosskonzerte.at) as

ENTERTAINMENT

well as in the fortress' lofty Golden Hall (www.mozartfestival.at). For either venue, check online or at the TI for schedule. **Note:** Concerts at Mirabell Palace cost 37€ (reserved seats, row 1-5) and 31€ (open seating from row 6) per adult or 18€ student, youth 9yr and younger 12€. If you buy your ticket through an agency there will be a surcharge of around 3€ per ticket. To beat the surcharge, buy direct from the palace ticket office located next to Mozart's Wohnhaus at Theatergasse 2 (walk through main door then second door on left, typically Mon-Fri 9:00-18:00, tel. 0662/848-586), or you can make your purchase at the Marble Hall starting one hour before the concert begins (but by this time the concert may already be sold out!).

Folks who are inspired by **organ concerts** (see TI for the various recitals planned around town or) check out the latest schedule at the Franciscan church (Franziskanerkirche with pointy tower and sheer roof soaring between the cathedral and festival halls), where there's usually an uplifting symphony of flue pipes summoning all angels.

S pend a fascinating afternoon/evening in the grand Baroque **Marionette Theater** (www.marionetten.at, tel. 0662/872-406, located at Schwarzstrasse 24, adjacent to the Mirabell Gardens and one block from the 5-star Hotel Sacher). Watch clever puppeteers nimbly manipulate small wooden people to dance and lip-sync and act like super humans not bound by gravity, bouncing and sometimes even levitating on stage. The string puppets and the art of their skillful masters are, to say the least, captivating to behold. Their repertoire includes big-time theatrical productions such as Mozart's "The Magic Flute," Shakespeare's "Midsummer Night's Dream," Brothers Grimm "Snow White and the Seven Dwarfs," Carroll's "Alice in Wonderland," and Humperdinck's "Hänsel and Gretel." (**Note:** The latter productions run about two hours and are performed to recordings by distinguished orchestras, singers and vocalists in their original language with English subtitles. Performances are scheduled a few times per week in May and most every day June-Sept; the remainder of the year the theater company is on tour entertaining audiences across the globe.)

©Salzburg Marionette Theater

Historically, the Salzburg Marionette Theater was founded by Anton Aicher in 1913 in a gymnasium near the Mirabell Gardens, where it remained for 49 years. At the start of World War II, the marionettes were sent to the front (first Norway then Russia) to entertain troops. The war tragically dragged on and the theater company was forced to close late 1944. Immediately after the war, 1945, the puppets were back in business entertaining American soldiers. In 1962, the theater company moved across the river to an auditorium near the cathedral on Kapitalplatz. In 1963, Hollywood contacted the puppeteers and the Lonely Goatherd sequence for the movie "The Sound of Music" was born. Finally, in 1971, the Salzburg marionettes found their present and permanent home (back across the river) at Schwarzstrasse 24, adjacent to the Mirabell Gardens.

In 2013, the Salzburg Marionette Theater proudly celebrated its 100-year birthday! Over the decades the theater has achieved mountains of success but in 2007 it perhaps landed its biggest industry coup with the purchase of the rights to perform the Broadway musical, "**The Sound of Music**." With this pricey acquisition a new stage backdrop had to be created along with a small army of intricately carved puppets. Because the marionettes cannot change their costumes, most members of the Trapp family had to be fashioned thrice. The 21 puppets, for example, representing the captain's seven children

GOOD EATS

posed a stringy challenge for the 10 puppeteers working the musical. After months of rehearsal, the curtain opened with great fanfare on the European premiere of the "The Sound of Music" at the Salzburg Marionette Theater on May 9, 2008; and I look forward to its success for seasons to come. So you can better plan your chance to see the von Trapp puppets in action, I've listed the musical's **2015 Salzburg schedule** (show duration 105 min; show times ¹17:00, *19:30): May *8, *15, *22, *29; **June** *5, *9, *12, *16, *19, *23, *26, *30; **July** *2, *3, *7, *9, *10, *14, *16, *17, *21, *23, *24, *28, *30, *31; **August** *4, ¹6, *7, *11, ¹13, *14, *18, ¹20, *21, *25, ¹27, *28; **September** *1, *4, *8, *9, *11, *15, *16, *18, *22, *23, *25.

    Prices at the Marionette Theater are the same for all (full-length) performances and you have a choice between four seating categories: **I** (35€, rows 1-9); **II** (30€, rows 10-14); **III** (25€, rows 15-20); **IV** (20€, row 21 and two sets of side seats opposite row 9), youth 12yr and under 15€. All major CCs accepted. Buy tickets online, at the theater box office (Mon-Sat 9:00-13:00 and two hours before every performance), or over the phone (0662/872-406 same hours as box office). If you purchase your ticket(s) online, avoid the "shipping" fee by picking up your ticket(s) at the box office. **Suggestion:** Because the puppets are small creatures, sit as close to the stage as your budget allows, thus anything in category I is fine. Rows 10-13 in category II are also respectable but row 14 is the first one beginning the second section to the back (which is ideal for tall folks seeking legroom) but it is also where the stage and puppets start becoming distant and I had to occasionally squint. If only row 14 is available from category II, consider saving the five euros per seat and opt for row 15 or 16 in category III (then if the theater's not full, move forward). The same strategy applies to seats 1, 2, 3, 4, 6 and 7 in row 21 (category IV). But the best value are the two (category IV) side seats (called Nische) opposite row 9 (but be quick because there are only four of these seats total, two either side of theater). Avoid rows 17-20 unless you're okay about the likelihood of confusing Hänsel with Gretel.

RESTAURANTS, CAFÉS, KEBABS & CURRY SAUSAGES

I begin this section by making a general statement that will always apply in my opinion regarding customary cuisine in Austria: "It's difficult to find a bad meal." People often ask, "Where's a good place to eat?" My answer sounds as if I'm shrugging them off: "Anywhere traditional." With that said, below are a few appetizing places to kick-start your gastronomic tour of Salzburg. (Vegetarians, try Spicy Spices on page 49.)

    But first, here's a short description of **Salzburger Nockerl** (pictured). Salzburger what? You'll see this dish on menus in the finer, traditional-style restaurants around town

(for example at St. Peter's Stiftskeller). It refers to a classic local dessert; a soufflé consisting of whipped egg whites and yolks, sugar, flour, lemon peel, vanilla, milk and butter beat into stiff mountain-like peaks served hot out-of-the-oven. Nockerl is airy yet filling, enough for three people, thus order one to share with your companion(s). And since it is prepared upon your request, never order one if you're in a hurry! It's not uncommon to wait 30 min for your specially made, sweet tasting meringue to arrive at your table.

    Lastly, if you're traveling in Salzburgland (or most anywhere in Germany) mid-April thru May, you'll be happy to know it's **Spargelzeit**, or "asparagus season." And like most resident kitchens, the majority of restaurants celebrate this spring time of year by complementing their dishes with the in-season specialty: white asparagus, harvested in a field near you as Spargel. I say "white" because these medium-length stalks of asparagus are pulled out of the ground (by hand) before reaching sunlight and turning green, the color we most associate with asparagus. Along your journey, you've likely seen Spargel for sale in bunches at markets and roadside stands. Spargel is typically boiled and served with any manner of sauces or seasonings to time-honored palate-pleasing perfection. So, if it's Spargelzeit, ask your waiter for a sampling of the succulent spear-shaped vegetable.

St. Peter's Stiftskeller, (16€-27€ main dish, tel. 0662/841-2680, daily 11:30-15:30 & 17:30-23:00 [kitchen 12:00-14:30 & 18:00-21:15], www.stpeter-stiftskeller.at, all major CCs accepted, English menu available, GPS: N47 47.832 E13 02.644). Located on the grounds of St. Peter's monastery and administered by the church, this sizeable 1,200-year-old restaurant with its various vaulted rooms undoubtedly needs to be mentioned first since it has been in business for ages, literally. The court scribe Alcuin first recorded the Stiftskeller, or monastic cellar, into the history books during a visit by Emperor Charlemagne in the year 803 A.D.; thus it is regarded as **Central Europe's oldest restaurant**! The prices are reasonable, the cuisine delectable, the setting historically unique, and the ambiance divine. Stop by for a bite to eat, even if it's only a soup or dessert (like the Salzburger Nockerl, a Stiftskeller specialty). Consider spending an evening here listening to poetic strains of Mozart over dinner (page 43).

Stieglkeller, (10€-19€ main dish, daily 11:00-23:00 (Jan./March closed Mon-Tue and all of Feb.), kitchen from 11:30, tel. 0662/842-681, www.stieglkeller.at, CC: VC,

MC). All over town you've probably seen the word "Stiegl," the name of Salzburg's beer and brewery, established in 1492. In 1820, the brewery expanded its revenue base by investing in the voluminous Stieglkeller restaurant, having multiple themed halls and a beer garden nestled above the rooftops of Salzburg (built into fortress hill at Festungsgasse 10, up from the cable railway). If the weather is nice, climb the cobbled lane and broad stone staircase to indulge in a traditional Austrian meal complemented by a thirst-quenching Stiegl beer and precious views from the Biergarten. Arrive before sunset and watch the Old Town transcend from the sun's golden rays reflecting off church steeples to the mesmeric twinkling of nocturnal lights.

Gasthaus zum Wilden Mann, (main dish from 10€, Mon-Sat 11:00-22:30 but kitchen till 21:00, tel. 0662/841-787, cash only—no CCs accepted). Secreted in a pedestrian passage off Getreidegasse, this rustic inn grows from lively locals hungry for something suggestive of their mother's kitchen and Stiegl beer on tap. Patrons share wooden tables while lederhosen-clad Robert (pictured) and his dirndl-donning partner Eva-Maria hustle delicious Austrian meals in ample portions from 10€. Popular choices are the beef stew with dumpling (Gulasch mit Knödel 10.50€), and the farmers' favorite Bauernschmaus (12.90€) containing roast pork, ham, sausage, dumplings, potatoes and sauerkraut. For

dessert, try the rolled pancakes with nuts and chocolate sauce and whipped cream (Scho-konuss Palatschinken 5.90€) or the apple strudel with vanilla sauce (4.50€). **To get there**, when facing Mozart's birthplace on Getreidegasse, go right to No. 22 (right). Proceed through the archway and down to Wilden Mann (left). Or, from Griesgasse (i.e. bus transportation hub at Hanuschplatz), enter the passage via the archway at No. 17.

Zum Fideln Affen, (12€-18€ main dish, Mon-Sat 17:00-midnight, tel. 0662/877-361, CC: VC, MC, AE). At this popular, non-smoking historic gasthaus (dating from circa 1650) kitchen chefs prepare each meal with art-like presentation (from ingredients

supplied by local farmers) while guests share wooden tables wrapped around a service bar and indulge in authentic Austrian cuisine that is plate-licking good! Zum Fideln Affen, local jargon meaning "To the Merry Monkey," is a cosy, convivial place with limited seating and hours, thus to arrive *without* a reservation would be akin to being a monkey's uncle. Savory suggestions include the wiener schnitzel and potatoes, tafelspitz (boiled beef) with veges, the multi-layered monkey (Affen) steak, and the delightful pumpkin-cream soup (Kürbiscremesuppe) served in a preservatives jar (seasonal thus try in the fall). But, beware, the bread rolls and pretzels kept irresistibly in front of you cost a pretty penny (inquire before indulging). **To get there**, zum Fideln Affen is located at Priesterhausgasse 8 in the New Town, across from the Star Inn hotel. Head up Linzergasse to No. 14 then jog left to the Affen ahead on the right.

Bärenwirt, (11€-17€ main dish, daily 11:00-23:00, kitchen 11:30-14:00 & 17:30-21:15, tel. 0662/422-404, CC: VC, MC). In the year 1562 it is said a black bear amazingly swam up from the river and rested here on the bank, thus today's storied Bärenwirt (Bear Inn) on Bärengässchen (Bear Lane) in the district of Mülln. Although the bear is long gone, its legacy lives on in this historic Wirtshaus (Inn) and its authentic Austrian fare, favored by locals. Dishes are prepared in large portions by generous chefs: start with the frothy beer soup (4.30€), or goulash soup (4.90€), then consider the wild boar sausage served with potatoes and cabbage in a skillet (11.90€), the Bärenwirt schnitzel (13.90€), the roast pork (Bierschopfbratl) with sauerkraut and a bread dumpling practically the size of a bear's head (11.80€), or the house specialty: fried chicken, said to be Austria's best! Wash it down with freshly tapped Augustiner beer served in a stoneware mug and brewed in the neighboring Müllner Bräu. The trick here is to leave room for dessert. **To get there**, Bärenwirt is located at Müllner Hauptstrasse 8, about a 20-min walk north along the river from the Old Town. **By bus** from Hanuschplatz (catch bus on river side heading north), ride either 7, 8, 20, 21, 27 (also departs from main train station direction Airport), or 28 one stop to "Bärenwirt." Exit bus left and go straight to the restaurant just ahead. **Drivers**, park three hours free at Müllner Bräu (Lindhofstrasse 7) around the corner from Bärenwirt—take ticket at gate and have your waiter validate it. **Note:** Combine a visit here with the Müllner Bräu (page 42). To get there from the Bärenwirt, exit the restaurant right and make the first left (across street) up cobbled Augustinergasse. At the top of the lane enter below the sign "Augustiner Bräustübl," then step through the last door on the left and skip down the stairway to heaven.

"Café-Restaurant," (daily 10:00-17:00, summer till 20:00, English menu available). Located at Festungsgasse 2, meters from the Stieglkeller (page 46), this casual eatery run by hard-working Helmut affords its guests pocket-friendly prices, a picture menu, and an ivy-swathed patio-garden with fortress view best on warm days. As you stroll up cobbled Festungsgasse toward the fortress, look for Helmet's sign advertising his lunch special: soup, schnitzel and potatoes (Kartoffel) 8.90€.

👍 **Troja (kebabs),** (Tue-Sat 20:00 thru 05:00, Giselkai 15—along river in New Town, some 7-8 doors south of Hotel Stein). Salzburg's yummiest kebabs (kebaps) can only be had nights and early mornings at the whole-in-the-wall Troja grill. Kebabs are 3.80€ but pay the extra .80¢ for the Dürüm wrapped like a burrito.

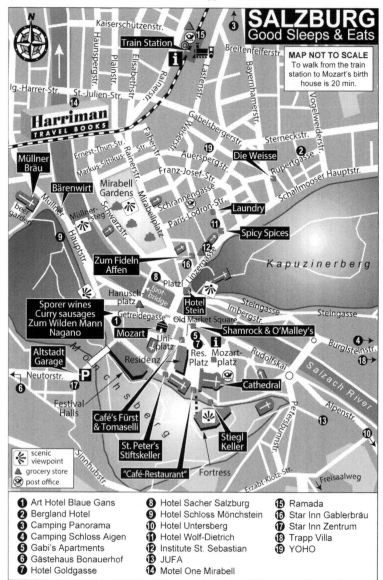

SALZBURG
Good Sleeps & Eats

MAP NOT TO SCALE
To walk from the train station to Mozart's birth house is 20 min.

Kapuzinerberg

Salzach River

scenic viewpoint
▲ grocery store
post office

GOOD EATS

❶ Art Hotel Blaue Gans
❷ Bergland Hotel
❸ Camping Panorama
❹ Camping Schloss Aigen
❺ Gabi's Apartments
❻ Gästehaus Bonauerhof
❼ Hotel Goldgasse
❽ Hotel Sacher Salzburg
❾ Hotel Schloss Mönchstein
❿ Hotel Untersberg
⓫ Hotel Wolf-Dietrich
⓬ Institute St. Sebastian
⓭ JUFA
⓮ Motel One Mirabell
⓯ Ramada
⓰ Star Inn Gablerbräu
⓱ Star Inn Zentrum
⓲ Trapp Villa
⓳ YOHO

Nagano restaurant (daily 11:30-15:00 & 17:00-23:00, tel. 0662/849-488) is centrally located, dishing up Japanese meals by Chinese staff from 11€ for those who are looking to escape pork and potatoes. Try their tasteful beer: Sapporo, Kirin, or Asahi. Order a small sake to share; it tastes like warm water but it's part of the experience. **Note:** Lunch specials typically Mon-Fri 11:00-14:30. **To get there**, when facing Mozart's birthplace on Getreidegasse, go right some 50 meters to No. 24 (right). Proceed through the archway and Nagano is beyond the second passage (right). Or, from Griesgasse (i.e. bus transportation hub at Hanuschplatz), enter the passage via the archway at No. 19a and Nagano is on the left.

Spicy Spices "Bio Bistro", (vegetarian and organic foods, daily special around 7€, Mon-Fri 11:30-21:00, Sat/Sun 12:00-21:00, Wolf-Dietrich-Strasse 1, top of Linzergasse, tel. 0662/870-712, <u>GPS</u>: N47 48.260 E13 02.906). The piquant aroma of herbs and spices tastefully fill the air in this petite family run Indian bistro (effectively a restaurant within a shop), an excellent choice for vegetarians or anyone looking for a healthy, steam-cooked meal with lentils. The owner takes pride in the government-issued certificate hanging on the wall guaranteeing that only the best-quality organic ("Bio") foods are used. Heck, you'll even find organic beer and juices on the menu to wash down all the Bio scrumptiousness, like naan chapati bread, panir cheese and lentil dal, tofu specialties, soya with peas, and most popular the **daily special**: typically a large Basmati or natural rice dish with vegetables in mild-curry sauce (add a fresh salad or soup for about 1.50€).

Shrimps Bar & Restaurant—11€-*29€ main dish, *surf and turf, daily 17:00-midnight, later Fri/Sat but kitchen closed by 22:30, located at Steingasse 5 behind Hotel Stein, tel. 0662/874-484, www.shrimps.at—newly renovated in 2013, has been serving a cross between Asian-fusion and Mediterranean-influenced salads, pastas and seafood specialties for over 30 years to the penchant of its fashionable customer base. Shrimps, true to its name, is a small, stylish establishment seating about 39, thus a reservation is suggested (and wholly recommended on weekends). With welcoming weather, choose a table outside and enjoy the best of Shrimps amidst the medieval charm of cobbled Steingasse that fronts the restaurant. Inside, soft lighting coupled with candlelit tables (most with a view to the chef preparing the dishes) and ambient background music strike the right mood to go with your meal. After dinner, consider a stroll across the lane for a nightcap on the Stein Terrasse (page 38).

Ikarus: Here 5-star cuisine is served in the company of billionaire *Dietrich Mateschitz's vintage aircraft collection at Salzburg airport (for more on Ikarus, see Hangar-7 page 34). *Founder of the Red Bull energy drink.

Stein Terrasse: This penthouse **café** is a must-visit, if only for a quick picture and a cuppa (page 38).

Café Fürst: Home to the original Mozart ball, locally Mozartkugel, Café Fürst outshines the bunch. Stop in for homemade chocolates, pastries, cakes and classic Austrian coffeehouse tradition. Café Fürst's flagship operation is located in the Old Town on Old Market Square (Alter Markt, neighboring Residenzplatz, Mon-Sat 8:00-20:00, Sun 9:00-20:00, www.original-mozartkugel.com, tel. 0662/843-7590, all major CCs accepted). Fürst has another, much smaller, location at Getreidegasse 47 (west end of pedestrian lane, Mon-Sat 10:00-18:30, Sun 11:00-17:00) as well as a third location across the river at Mirabellplatz 5 (Mon-Fri 9:00-19:00, Sat-Sun 9:00-18:00), opposite Mirabell Gardens. For more on the original Mozart ball, see page 39.

SHRIMPS
BAR UND RESTAURANT

GOOD EATS

Café Tomaselli, (Mon-Sat 7:00-20:00, Sun 8:00-20:00, summer till 21:00, mid-July thru Aug till 22:00, tel. 0662/844-4880, <u>cash only</u>). Austria's oldest coffeehouse,

dating from 1703, Café Tomaselli set up shop not long after retreating Turkish soldiers hastily left sacks of coffee beans on the battlefield outside Vienna. Over the centuries Tomaselli's has seen many distinguished persons walk through its doors, including celebrities, politicians, artists, and one very famous composer: Wolfgang Amadeus, whose preferred drink here was said to be 'almond milk.' (Even Mozart's widow Constanze lived above the café from 1820-26.) Inside, pastry waitresses wearing kitchen-maid uniforms and tuxedo-clad waiters serve customers who sit contentedly on wooden chairs positioned around marble-topped tables, sipping coffee, eating cake, chatting, *smoking, reading, people watching—the setting here is comparable to a 19th-century oil painting by Édouard Manet. Step into Tomaselli's storied ambiance and be a part of the scene. (*Note: Non-smoking areas include the room adjoining the main café area as well as upstairs.) Keeping to tradition, Wi-Fi is trumped here by the old-and-reliable newspaper rack in the corner respectfully squeaking with every twirl commanded by customers seeking the latest domestic and international publications. The adjacent staircase climbs to the best seats in the house on the terrace; you're in luck if a table is available (you can also reach the terrace via the outdoor staircase right of the café spiraling up from the square). Plop down and relish life. Order your beverage from the waiter then select a delectable dessert from the Kuchenmädchen (pastry waitress) making the rounds with the homemade sweets finely presented on a sterling-silver tray. **To get there**, look for Tomaselli's signature green-and-white table umbrellas fronting the storied café on Old Market Square (Alter Markt) across from the above-listed Café Fürst.

Café Classic, (www.cafeclassic.at, Mon-Sat 8:00-19:30, Sun also mid-July thru Aug, Makartplatz 8, tel. 0662/ 882-700, CC: VC, MC). Directly next door to Mozart's Wohnhaus (page 26), consider a break at this "classic" coffeehouse not only for its specialty beverages and pastries and refined atmosphere but also for its daily food specials that make this café a sensible stop for lunch or any-time snack.

Curry Sausages at the Bosna Grill, (Mon-Fri 11:00-19:00, Sat 11:00-17:00, and July-Dec also Sun 16:00-20:00, but don't wait until the last minute because they often sell out and close early!). Arguably Salzburg's favorite sausage has Bulgarian origins and can be found at the Bosna Grill, a literal whole in the wall since 1950. You typically won't find many tourists here, mostly locals waiting in line to take away a spicy and fatty taste of bliss prepared with special seasonings secreted in a time-honored recipe. The person working behind the window (with little more than elbow room to move) proudly serves up the so-called "Bosna": two sausages jammed in a hot-dog-like bun dripping with condiments. You have five choices, 3.40€ each: **1)** with onions and curry spice • **2)** with onions, curry spice and mustard • **3)** with mustard and curry spice • **4)** with onions, ketchup and curry spice • **5)** with ketch-

up and curry spice. **To get there,** when facing Mozart's birthplace on Getreidegasse, go right to No. 33 (left). Proceed through the archway into the cobbled passage to the whole in the wall some 10 meters ahead on the right.

　　Café-Restaurant Stadtalm, (daily from April 10:00-18:00, May till 19:00-22:00, June-Aug till 23:00, but closed during bad weather, tel. 0662/841-729, www.di-estadtalm.com). Here you can eat and drink high above the Old Town in a medieval watchtower or outside on one of the umbrellaed picnic tables parked along the cliff's edge where sweeping views of Salzburg come with the (sometimes poor) service. Nestled upon the Mönchsberg (Monks' Ridge), Stadtalm is part of the city's historic defense wall built by the citizen guard in 1487. Hike the forested Mönchsberg and make the reasonably priced Stadtalm part of your adventure, if only for a glass of my favorite beer: Wieninger (3.10€/0.5l). Budget-minded travelers with few bags may be interested in Stadtalm's bunk-bed lodgings (from 21.50€/B&B), affording first-class views for a pauper's price and hallway toilets-showers. **To get there,** GPS: N47 47.977 E13 02.357, look above the northwest part of the Old Town for a wood-covered duct leading up the cliff face—the battlement at the top is the Stadtalm. Ride the Lift (page 31) up Mönchsberg then read Mönchsberg Lift & Hiking Trails (page 38).

GOOD SLEEPS

In this pedestrianized city of salt there are more accommodations than you can poke a stick at. Not that I endorse stick poking, or any other poking of sorts. Below is an abridged list of restful lodgings to simplify, from cheap to steep, both for **Railers** and **Drivers** (the latter found in the latter half of this Good Sleeps section). Unless otherwise noted, all accommodations come with breakfast and have a shower and toilet in the room, excluding hostels (and of course the two campgrounds listed at the very end of this section).

　　To help you better navigate this section, I've rated each accommodations entry with a dollar symbol based on the price of **double occupancy.** For example, one $ symbol means the price of a double (twin) at the respective property is 60€ or less; two $$ symbols mean the price of a double (twin) is generally between 60€ and 100€; three $$$ symbols mean the price is generally between 100€ and 170€; four $$$$ symbols mean the price exceeds 180€.

> $ — pocket-friendly, 60€ or less
> $$ — moderately priced, generally between 60€ and 100€
> $$$ — upper end, generally between 100€ and 170€
> $$$$ — superior, from 180€

Note: Room prices throughout town typically increase a great deal during the 45-day Salzburg Festival, mid-July thru August. As you already know from reading the beginning of this chapter, I urge you to buy the Salzburg Card (page 9)—which also may be for sale at your accommodations. Note that when "dbl" is written below it refers to a private room for two persons, not necessarily a private room having a double bed. Typically in Austria a double bed is two singles, or twins, pushed together to form a double. If it is a twin you're after, request when booking that the beds be separated.

　　The weather in Salzburg rarely sizzles in summer but in case you arrive during a heat wave, you risk a sleepless night due to the open windows in your room amplifying the possible street racket like bullhorns at a union rally, unless of course your accommodations are **air-conditioned**. The following digs from this section have AC: Star Inn

(Gablerbräu and Zentrum pages 54 & 61), Motel One (page 54), Ramada (page 55), Art Hotel Blaue Gans (page 58), Hotel Sacher and Hotel Schloss Mönchstein (pages 58-59).

Budget-minded travelers seeking a private room should also consider the hostels YoHo (see below) and JUFA (page 53).

Railers, from the main train station, the Ramada is located next door and the YoHo hostel is a 10-min walk. All the rest are within a 30-min walk or, easier, reachable via bus. **Drivers**, digs more suitable to you are listed in the latter half of this Good Sleeps section, beginning on page 60.

Families, consider the following digs which offer rooms conducive to parties of 3 or more persons: YoHo (page 52); JUFA (page 53); Star Inn Gablerbräu (page 54); Star Inn Zentrum (Drivers, page 61); Hotel Wolf-Dietrich (page 56); Art Hotel Blaue Gans (page 58); Gästehaus Bonauerhof (kids love to play with the animals here, Drivers, page 60); Bergland Hotel (Drivers, page 62).

$ (hostel) **YoHo,** (Paracelsusstrasse 9, a 15-min walk from the Old Town, tel. 0662/ 879-649, www.yoho.at, **free Wi-Fi** in lobby or use of Internet computer for 1.50€/hr). If you're looking for a hostel with a lively atmosphere, look no further. YoHo is the No. 1 choice in town for backpackers, affording its guests friendly staff, discounted tours, bike rental, laundry facilities, daily screening of the movie "**The Sound of Music**" (at 19:00), inexpensive meals (breakfast buffet 3.50€, dinner 19:00-20:30), movies and Nintendo Wii console on loan from reception, and an in-house bar with a very "happy hour" (usually 2€ beer/wine 18:00-19:00 & again 22:00-23:00). **PRICE**, (summer rates quoted, less

off-season; sheets and key included but require a 5€ deposit), 8-bed dorm 20€, 6-bed 21€, 4-bed 22€ (24€ with shower in room), Sgl from 41€, Dbl from 67€, family room possible. CC: VC, MC. **Note:** Check-in from 12:00, check-out by 10:00. GPS: N47 48.496 E13 02.848. **Drivers**, street parking where space is available (free weekends or Mon-Fri 1.30€/hr 9:00-19:00 max 3hr); discounted garage parking possible (see reception). **Railers**, from the main train station YoHo is roughly 7€ by taxi or a

10-min walk. By foot, exit front of station and go left some 200 meters to the traffic light, then walk left through the tunnel. Continue straight and make the second right into Paracelsusstrasse. Your digs are on the second block, right side. **From Salzburg airport**, a taxi will cost around 16€ (depending on traffic), or hop on bus 2 toward town and get off at Stelzhamerstrasse, 30-min ride (5th stop after main train station, push button on handrail to signal driver to stop; bus departs every 10 min, and every 20 min after 19:00 Mon-Sat and all day Sun)—exit bus left then make the first left (Lasserstrasse), at the forward intersection go left again and cross the street to your digs.

$$ (hostel) **Institute St. Sebastian,** (Linzergasse 41, 5-min walk from the Old Town, www.st-sebastian-salzburg.at, tel. 0662/871-386, reception typically open daily 8:00-12:00 & 16:00-21:00 but longer in summer, charge for **Wi-Fi**). Incomparable hostel, clean facilities and centrally located, Institute St. Sebastian doubles as a home for college students, thus it has all the necessary amenities to sustain long-term occupancy, e.g. elevator, self-service kitchens, laundry facility (book at reception, about 4€/load), communal rooms, and a peaceful rooftop terrace. What's more, St. Sebastian's is oozing with history (thus the reason I used the word "incomparable" above) because it adjoins a late-Gothic church built in 1505 and the hostel's backyard is an enchanting cemetery

(page 32), landscaped in 1595. Eternal inhabitants include Mozart's father, Leopold (d. 1787) and Mozart's widow, Constanze Weber (d. 1842). **PRICE** (includes sheets, buffet breakfast), dorm bed 24€, Sgl from 48€, Dbl from 68€, Trpl from 105€, quad 118€. CC: VC, MC. **Note:** If staying only one night add 5€/person to rate. Church bells begin ringing at 6:00! GPS: N47 48.231 E13 02.814. **By foot** from the Old Town, walk across the Salzach River via the Staatsbrücke (main bridge) and climb Linzergasse to No. 37, then swing left through the arch to reception just inside the door on the right. **Railers**, from the main train station, it's about a 25-min walk (take Rainerstrasse straight to Mirabellplatz then follow "Exit bus left…" directions), about 8€ with taxi, or take any bus direction Zentrum and get off at Mirabellplatz (3rd stop). **Exit bus left** and cross the street with the traffic light into Paris-Lodron-Strasse. Continue straight some 150 meters to the stone archway on the right, just past the Loreto church. Walk through the archway and continue straight through the passages. The door into the hostel will appear near the end on the left at No. 41 (before archway). **From Salzburg airport**, a taxi will cost around 19€ (tell the driver you want to be driven through the city [the alternative route is longer via the autobahn]), or hop on bus 2 toward town and get off at Mirabellplatz, 30-min ride (3rd stop after main train station; bus departs every 10 min, and every 20 min after 19:00 Mon-Sat and all day Sun), then follow the above directions for Railers: "Exit bus left…."

$$ (hostel-hotel) **JUFA,** short for Jugend & Familiegästehaus, (Josef-Preis-Allee 18, www.jufa.eu, tel. 05/708-3613, **free Wi-Fi** in lobby or use of Internet computer for purchase). This large 4-story youth-and-family hostel-hotel, located within easy reach of the Old Town (under 10 min by foot), has recently undergone major renovations that deserve your attention. The lobby is spacious and sunlit, inviting and airy, a place to make new friends, exchange ideas and stories, pick up the latest brochure, plan the day's itinerary or relax with a beverage from the café-bar, watch the movie "**The Sound of Music**" (free daily screening at 20:00, ask reception to start movie), log on to free wireless, or rent a bike to cycle along the river. Adjoining the lobby, the **cafeteria** offers a heaping dinner menu with vegan alternatives (18:00-20:00, around 7€ small plate or 10€ all-you-
can-eat buffet). Stop by; dig in. All told, this wheelchair-accessible hostel-hotel has 350 beds, an elevator, laundry (5€/load=wash-dry-powder), and large views to the fortress! ***PRICE** (includes sheets and an excellent breakfast buffet with scrambled eggs), 8-bed dorm from 20€, 6-bed from 22€, Sgl from 50€, Dbl from 83€, family room available. All major CCs accepted. **Note:** *Rates change regularly depending on availability. Check-in from 13:00. No common kitchen. All private rooms are outfitted with a shower and toilet. Individual travelers looking for a dorm bed only have the 6 & 8-bed options (which are small rooms located one level below ground with meager ventilation). Lockers are provided in the hallway and work with a 2€ deposit (coin is returned upon reopening locker). **Suggestion:** Devote an evening to the film classic "The Sound of Music." Have dinner here around 19:30 then watch the movie at 20:00. If you're not done with your meal by the time Maria takes to the hills, finish it in the TV lounge. To complement your von-Trapp experience: beer, soda, hot drinks, pizza, sandwiches, fruits, whatnot are available for purchase at the snack bar (note the vending machine downstairs sells half-liter sodas for about 1.40€). GPS: N47 47.689 E13 03.370. **Drivers**, park in JUFA lot out front of property, 5€/day. **Railers**, from the main train station, a taxi will cost around 9€, or ride either

bus 5 or 25 to Justizgebäude (10 min)—exit bus left and walk some 50 meters to the crosswalk (at traffic light) and cross over. On the other side of the road continue straight along Josef-Preis-Allee to your digs at the end. **From Salzburg airport**, a taxi will cost around 15€, or ride bus 2 from outside the airport to the Hauptbahnhof (main train station) then change buses to 5 or 25 (follow directions above for Railers).

$$ Motel One (Mirabell), (Elisabethkai 60, www.motel-one.com, tel. 0662/ 885-200, **free Wi-Fi** in room). Don't be misled by the name. This non-smoking budget-design hotel is such good value that I look forward to recommending the chain whenever possible across Europe, already having excellent locations in Berlin, Munich, Vienna, Brussels, Edinburgh, London, and Prague. Motel One is a new pocket-friendly hotel group that is true to its marketing slogan: Viel Design für Wenig Geld (meaning "a whole lotta design for little money"). No matter which Motel One you visit, the design and concept are the same. You can count on 24-hour reception; air-conditioning; free Wi-Fi; modish décor accented by the company's aqua-colored theme, starting with the stylish lobby to the trendy room furnishings, including a flat-screen TV, ceramic vessel sink in the bathroom and a soothing shower with "rain" showerhead. Opened December 2012, this Salzburg "Mirabell" property scenically sits alongside the Salzach River, between the main train station and Mirabell Gardens, a pleasant 15-min walk along the river to the Old Town. **Important:** All odd-numbered rooms have river views and even-numbered rooms face the ugly apartment block across the back lane, thus be sure to request a river view. **PRICE**, Sgl 69€, Dbl 84€, Dbl with balcony 104€ (hotel has only nine of these room-types—note that in this room buttons on wall lower/raise window shade), buffet breakfast 9.50€. All major CCs accepted. **Note:** Check-in from 15:00, check-out by 12:00. Rooms are rather small. One child up to 12yr is free in parents' room; child up to 6yr receives free breakfast to boot. During special events and the 45-day Salzburg Festival July-August, add 20€-50€ to the room rate. **Drivers**, in-house parking, 12€/day. Unload out front and notify reception. **Railers**, from the main train station, Motel One Mirabell is roughly 7€ by taxi, a 10-min walk, or catch *bus 1 (direction Messe/Arena) or *bus 2 (direction Airport/Walserfeld—*departing every 10 min, and every 20 min after 19:00 Mon-Sat and all day Sun) and get off at St. Julien Strasse (2nd stop) to your digs across the busy road. **From Salzburg airport**, a taxi will cost around 15€ (depending on traffic), or hop on bus 2 toward town and get off at St. Julien Strasse to your digs across the busy road (20-min ride, push button on handrail to signal driver to stop; bus departs every 10 min, and every 20 min after 19:00 Mon-Sat and all day Sun).

$$ Star Inn Gablerbräu, (Richard-Mayr-Gasse 2, a short walk across the river from Mozart's birthplace, tel. 0662/879-662, www.starinnhotels.com, **free Wi-Fi** in room). Located in the heart of New Town, a stone's throw from the Old Town, this freshly renovated (May 2012) 3-star property in the econo-class Star Inn family adds 77 air-conditioned rooms in varying categories (from standard to business superior, suites and apartments) with modern design, queen-sized beds, and flat-screen TVs to Salzburg's heaping accommodations pool. Unlike its "Zentrum" sister property (page 61), these centrally located digs afford its guests the option of apartments with kitchen and one sweet rooftop suite! First documented in 1429 (then a brew house under a different name), the storied Gablerbräu property boasts a rich tradition of serving its Salzburg clientele. **PRICE**, standard Sgl from 84€ (biz 104€, suite 124€); standard Dbl from 104€ (biz 124€, suite 144€); Trpl from 134€; quad/family from 144€; rooftop suite (up to 4 pers.) from 199€; breakfast buffet 13€/person. All major CCs accepted. **Note:** Reception open 24 hours. Two children up to the age of 11 accompanied by their parents stay for free, including breakfast (if parents booked their own). During the 45-day Salzburg Festival mid-July thru August and Advent, add 60€/night to the room rates (and 100€ for the roof-top suite). Reception sells the Salzburg Card, tours, and concert/event tickets. **Railers**, from the main train station, it's around a 20-min walk, around 9€ with taxi (depending on traffic), or catch bus 1, 3, 5, 6 or 25 direction Zentrum and get off at Makartplatz (4th stop)—exit bus right and at the top of the street go right across the cross walk straight into Dreifaltigkeitsgasse, then make the first left into Richard-Mayr-Gasse to your digs ahead on the right. **From Salzburg airport**, a taxi will cost around 15€ (depending on traffic), or ride bus 2 from outside the airport to the Hauptbahnhof (main train station) then change buses (follow directions above for Railers). **Drivers**, tough to reach due to one-way streets and pedestrian zones, get directions from reception in advance. Unload out front and get the discount voucher from reception to the Mirabell garage on Mirabell-platz (5-min walk), about 15€/day.

$$ Star Inn Zentrum, (page 61). The sister property to the above-listed Ga-blerbräu, Star Inn Zentrum works well for both Drivers and Railers, thus I've placed its listing here as well as in the second part of the Good Sleeps section for Drivers.

$$ Ramada, (Südtiroler Platz 13, www.ramada.com, tel. 0662/22850, toll-free res-ervations from USA/Canada 1-800-854-9517 or within Austria 0800/201-478, within Germany 0800/181-9098, **free Wi-Fi** and use of Internet computer in lobby). Positioned within a 6-floor glass tower next to the main train station, these non-smoking digs are most convenient for luggage-weary Railers in search of accommodations bang on the doorstep of local transportation (buses, taxis, trains) journeying people here and there, including to all the sights *and* Berchtesgaden. Moreover, meters away is a supermarket, pharmacy, and the TI. Opened May 2008, this Ramada offers 120 small yet modern air-conditioned rooms, each with a flat-screen TV but oddly without a mini-bar fridge. Enjoy a breakfast buffet on the scenic sixth-floor in view of the dramatic Salzburger Alps, fortress and church steeples. To reach the Old Town from the Ramada is either a 20-min walk (have reception point you the way) or catch bus 3, 5, 6 or 25 direction Zentrum and get off at Rathaus (5th stop). **PRICE**, Sgl/Dbl from 89€ (book online at least three days in advance and save 10%), breakfast buffet 16€/person. All major CCs accepted. **Note:** Check-in from 15:00, check-out by 11:00. Toiletries available at reception. One youth (17yr or younger) allowed per room with adult free of charge. If required, porter service is available for a fee (notify reception). During the 45-day Salzburg Festival mid-July thru August, add roughly 25% to the room rate. **Railers**, exit main train station right into your digs. **From Salzburg airport**, a taxi will cost around 15€ (tell the driver you want to be driven through the city [the alternative route is longer via the autobahn]), or hop on bus 2 toward town and get off at the Hauptbahnhof (main train station), 20-min ride (bus departs every 10 min, and every 20 min after 19:00 Mon-Sat and all day Sun). **Drivers**, parking around 14€/24hr, follow signs to Zentrum then Hauptbahnhof.

$$$ Gabi's Apartments, (Brodgasse 3, www.salzburgplacetostay.com, email: apartments@sp2s.com, **free Wi-Fi** in room). Experience the romantic flavor and medieval charm of Salzburg in one of Gabi's self-contained apartments, which are won-derfully located in the heart of the Old Town. I mean, if Mozart were still alive, you'd call him *neighbor*. Elegantly furnished, these non-smoking, wood-beamed digs are so en-chanting you'll want to call them your own! The only drawback, the building in Brod-gasse dates from the 14th century (circa 1374) and the elevator-equivalent in those days is a stone staircase climbing some 80 steps to the apartments (I-IV) on the 4th floor. In-corporate this into an exercise program and reward yourself with an extra helping of strudel after dinner. Since all the apartments are self-contained, they include the 21st-century comforts of home, such as a kitchen, microwave, washer-dryer, refrigerator, Ne-

GOOD SLEEPS

spresso coffee maker, flat-screen TV, DVD player (Gabi has a limited selection of movies on loan, such as *The Sound of Music*), etc.—you only need to bring shampoo and soap. Oh, and bring your own recipes in case you decide to stay in for an evening and cook. In Salzburg Old Town, everything is synonymous with romantic, starting right here at Gabi's apartments! **PRICE**, cash only; Sgl/Dbl 110-120€ per apartment per night, (Trpl possible in apts I, II, IV & VI, add 40€/person), plus a 40€ cleaning/laundry fee per stay. **Note:** Minimum 3 nights required to stay. Payment is cash only—a 50% deposit in euro is required via PayPal and the remaining balance due upon arrival (but first email Gabi the dates you wish to stay and she'll reply to your query in perfect English). Deal: Stay 7 nights and pay 6! **Apartments:** Gabi has a total of six apartments, four of these (I, II, III, IV) are located at Brodgasse 3; a fifth apartment (V) with elevator and washer but *no* dryer is just  across the river in Linzergasse, a schnitzel toss from the Old Town; and in 2013 she added a sixth apartment (VI) to her exclusive collection, which is situated on the ground floor of a historic building in the Old Town between the cathedral and fortress. Apartment I is the biggest, thus 120€ per night. Apartments II-VI are 110€ per night, but note that apt. V has an elevator in the building (thus no leg workout is necessary to reach your room) and apt. III does not have a DVD player (thus if you were planning on watching a movie, such as *The Sound of Music*, be sure to tell Gabi so you don't get this room). Apartments do not have air-conditioning but instead have a fan. **Drivers**, for all apartments except V, park in Altstadt Garage "B," enter at Hildmannplatz 1, 18€/24hr. **Railers**, from the main train station, it's about a 25-min walk to the Brodgasse apartments (I-IV, for apartments V & VI get directions in advance from Gabi), around 9€ with taxi, or catch bus 3, 5, 6 or 25 direction Zentrum and get off at Rathaus (5th stop)—exit bus and take lane running beneath archway. Turn left ahead then go straight, keeping the square (Alter Markt) to your right, and make the first right to your digs meters ahead on the left. **From Salzburg airport**, a taxi will cost around 15€ (depending on traffic), or ride bus 10 toward town (departing every 15 min, every 30 min after 19:00 Mon-Sat and all day Sun) and get off at Rathaus (20-min ride), then follow the above directions for Railers: "—exit bus and take…." Another option, take the more frequent bus 2 from outside the airport to the Hauptbahnhof (main train station) then follow directions above for Railers.

$$$ Hotel Wolf-Dietrich, (Wolf-Dietrich-Strasse 7, www.salzburg-hotel.at, tel. 0662/871-275, **free Wi-Fi** in room and use of Internet computer in lobby). Located on a quiet street within a 10-min walk of Mirabell, Mozart and the Old Town, this stylish family friendly boutique hotel deserves every one of its 4 stars. Rooms are tastefully decorated, comfortable, practical and some even downright romantic, such as the themed suites with canopy beds and free-standing bathtubs. The hotel's 40 rooms are situated within two buildings: the **Altstadt** is the main building (with reception, spa, breakfast service, and elevator) and the **Residenz** is directly across the street (also with elevator but does not reach the top floor). Both properties are fine, each elegantly refurbished within a large historic row house. One of the many delights regarding the Wolf-Dietrich is its free amenities and services, such as the spa (daily 7:00-22:00, swimming pool, Finnish sauna, steam room); the complimentary tea-coffee-cake-fruit in the afternoon (15:30-

GOOD SLEEPS

18:00); the selection of organic foods at breakfast; daily international newspapers; and because all rooms have a DVD player you can borrow a DVD from the library of movies (like *The Sound of Music*) free of charge at reception. **PRICE** (includes breakfast buffet), standard Sgl 80-130€, Dbl 138-230€, romantic Dbl 178-218€, family room (up to 4 pers.) 188-310€, extra bed 25€. All major CCs accepted. **Note:** During the 45-day Salzburg Festival mid-July thru August and Advent, add 25-35% to the room rate. Vegetarians, try Spicy Spices (page 49) a few doors along. Convenient if you're in need of fresh clothes, the hotel has an in-house laundry service or you'll find a laundromat (Norge Exquisit Textilreinigung, Mon-Fri 7:30-18:00, Sat 8:00-12:00, last wash two hours before closing, 14€/load, pay attendant) parked on the corner of Paris-Lodron-Strasse. Around the other corner is St. Sebastian's Cemetery (page 32), grave site of Mozart's father and widow. GPS: N47 48.260 E13 02.906. **Drivers**, hotel parking 15€/day, unload out front then have reception point you to the nearby garage. **Railers**, from the main train station, a taxi will cost around 8€, or hop on bus 2 direction Zentrum/Obergnigl and get off at Wolf-Dietrich-Strasse (4th stop but push button on handrail to signal driver to stop; bus departs every 10 min, and every 20 min after 19:00 Mon-Sat and all day Sun). Exit bus right then go left on Wolf-Dietrich-Strasse to your digs ahead on the right. **From Salzburg airport**, a taxi will cost around 16€ (tell the driver you want to be driven through the city [the alternative route is longer via the autobahn]), or hop on bus 2 toward town and get off at Wolf-Dietrich-Strasse, 30-min ride (4th stop after main train station but push button on handrail to signal driver to stop; bus departs every 10 min, and every 20 min after 19:00 Mon-Sat and all day Sun). Exit bus right then go left on Wolf-Dietrich-Strasse to your digs ahead on the right.

$$$$ **Hotel Goldgasse,** (Goldgasse 10, www.hotelgoldgasse.at, tel. 0662/845-622, **free Wi-Fi**). Tucked onto a crooked pedestrian lane flanked by art and antique shops in the heart of the Old Town; at Hotel Goldgasse you'll get an authentic feel of Baroque life in Mozart's day. Really! Dating from the 14th century, the hotel is one of Salzburg's oldest inns, complete with a rich Austrian tradition and a venerated restaurant serving regional cuisine. That said, Hotel Goldgasse (formerly the Goldene Ente) changed ownership and underwent a complete renovation. Reopening December 2014, each of its 15 sophisticated rooms are individually outfitted with contemporary design elements, oak wood flooring, a marble bathroom, flat-screen TV, Italian SMEG minibar fridge, De-Longhi espresso machine, Nespresso capsules, and organic tea selections. Upon arriving, head to reception where Ulrike is routinely on duty and (as your cordial host) ready to welcome *you* to the new Hotel Goldgasse and sensational Salzburg! **PRICE** (breakfast *not* included), Sgl superior 98-160€ or Dbl as Sgl 120-180€, standard Dbl 165-260€, Jr suite 225-340€, apartment superior (4 pers.) 270-410€, extra bed 83€, breakfast 23€. CC: VC, MC. **Note:** Check-in from 14:00, check-out by 11:00. **Drivers**, park in Altstadt Garage "B," enter at Hildmannplatz 1, 18€/24hr. On foot, exit garage Festspielhäuser to Toskaninihof opening to the Old Town. **Railers**, from the main train station, it's about a 25-min walk, around 9€ with taxi, or catch bus 3, 5, 6 or 25 direction Zentrum and get off at Rathaus (5th stop)—exit bus and take the lane running beneath the archway. Turn left ahead then go straight, keeping the square (Alter Markt) to your right, make the first right then go left on Goldgasse to your digs ahead on the right. **From Salzburg airport**, a taxi will cost around 15€ (depending on traffic), or ride bus 10 toward town (departing every 15 min, every 30 min after 19:00 Mon-Sat and all day Sun) and get off at Rathaus (20-min ride), then follow the above directions for Railers: "—exit bus and take…." Another option, take the more frequent bus 2 from outside the airport to the Hauptbahnhof (main train station) then follow directions above for Railers.

$$$$ Art Hotel Blaue Gans, (Getreidegasse 43, www.blauegans.at, tel. 0662/8424-9150, **free Wi-Fi** in room and use of Internet computer in lobby). This trendy art hotel could hardly be better situated in the hub of the Old Town, on Salzburg's historic shopping street, Getreidegasse, meters from Mozart's birth house. The Blaue Gans, or Blue Goose, dates from the 16th century and, although the historical shell remains, these digs have been fully refurbished to an air-conditioned house of contemporary design studios for tasteful travelers like you and me to lay our heads. Rooms are minimalist yet bright and fashionable, a product of modern art, each individually created but similarly outfitted with flat-screen TVs and Wi-Fi. The hotel regularly hosts art exhibitions and social events, usually an in-vogue affair (like the time I stopped by to find the luxury car manufacturer Maserati holding a promotion for its latest GranTurismo). Adjoining the hotel is the recommended traditional-style Blaue Gans restaurant and next door to that is the intoxicating Sporer wines & spirits (page 40). **PRICE** (includes breakfast buffet), Sgl 135-209€, small Dbl (20 m²) 145-209€, regular Dbl 155-239€, medium Dbl (30 m²) 189-289€, large Dbl 229-339€, "city flat"/"festspiel suite" (80 m²) 269-399€, bi-level "maisonette suite" (115 m²) 359-499€, extra bed 40€ (6-12yr 20€, 0-5yr free). All major CCs accepted. **Note:** The lobby area is small; if the front desk is unattended upon your arrival, wait a minute and the receptionist will be right with you. The single, small double and regular double rooms are petite in size, thus opt for a medium double or larger room if your budget allows. **Railers**, from the main train station, a taxi will cost around 10€, or hop on bus 1 direction Zentrum (departs every 10 min, and every 20 min after 19:00 Mon-Sat and all day Sun) and get off at Herbert von Karajan Platz (3rd stop after crossing river but push button on handrail after 2nd stop, Mönchsbergaufzug, to signal driver to stop). Exit bus left, cross the street (left) with the traffic light, to your digs on the left (enter through back door and head straight to front desk). **From Salzburg airport**, a taxi will cost around 12€, or ride bus 10 toward town (departing every 15 min, every 30 min after 19:00 Mon-Sat and all day Sun) and get off at Herbert von Karajan Platz (15-min ride). Exit bus straight to your digs in front of you (enter through back door and head straight to front desk). Other than bus 10, another option would be to catch bus 2 outside the airport then connect onto bus 1, like so: ride bus 2 toward town (departing every 10-20 min until about 22:55) and get off a few stops later at Hans-Schmid-Platz (mention this to bus driver upon boarding). From here cross over to bus 1 direction Messe/Arena and get off after a handful of stops at Herbert von Karajan Platz (first stop after tunnel; push button on handrail to signal driver to stop). Exit bus straight to your digs in front of you (enter through back door and head straight to front desk). **Drivers**, (enter Herbert von Karajan Platz into your GPS navigation system), exit A1 autobahn at "Flughafen" and follow signs to Salzburg, then Mitte and Hotel route. After about 4 km you will reach a giant cliff face; drive through the tunnel and at the traffic light continue straight (into Herbert von Karajan Platz); pull into the first available space on the left to unload your bags. The outdoor café/restaurant belongs to the Blaue Gans; enter through back door and head straight to the front desk; have receptionist point you to the parking garage and explain the discounted 14€/24hr tariff.

$$$$ Hotel Sacher Salzburg, (Schwarzstrasse 7, www.sacher.com, tel. 0662/889-770, **free Wi-Fi** in room). Nestled on the right bank of the Salzach River and facing the Old Town, Hotel Sacher has a reputation of impeccable service, accommodations and tradition that far exceeds the boundaries of Austria. Since its grand opening in 1866 (then the Österreichischer Hof), Hotel Sacher's sumptuous 5-star digs have been a popular rendezvous for celebrities, royalty, jet-setting tycoons, political heavyweights,

GOOD SLEEPS

Hollywood movie stars, honeymooners, and free spirits like you and me who care to splurge once in awhile for that deserving occasion. Among Sacher's famous residents, Julie Andrews and director Robert Wise stayed here in 1964 during the filming of "The Sound of Music." Tom Hanks, the Dalai Lama, John Denver, Sylvester Stallone, Placido Domingo, and First Lady Hillary Clinton have also been guests at Hotel Sacher, an esteemed property belonging to The Leading Hotels of the World (www.lhw.com). Individuality and personal service are top priorities at Hotel Sacher Salzburg, privately owned and run by the Gürtler family since 1988. Guests are welcome to indulge in his or her taste of luxury. Painstakingly planned by management and industry professionals, each

of Sacher's 113 rooms and suites have been individually decorated and are a showcase of precious antiques and Oriental rugs, silk wallpaper and original oil paintings. Delicate and soothing color schemes complement sophisticated design elements. Rooms are clean, sharp, spirited, homey, fashionable, air-conditioned, outfitted with flat-screen TVs and Wi-Fi and the latest sound systems. Savor the finest cuisine in Sacher's three restaurants; experience traditional Austrian coffeehouse culture at Café Sacher; or meet in the Sacher Bar (daily 11:00-01:00) and chill with a cocktail to the air of a live pianist (typically Mon-Sat beginning at 18:00). At Hotel Sacher, everything is possible: even a room facing the river and Old Town (which I recommend you request, the alternative is to face the busy road on which you arrived). **PRICE** (advance Internet rates quoted), standard Dbl from 190€, superior Dbl from 271€, deluxe Dbl from 355€, junior suite from 439€, suite from 896€, presidential suite from 2,500€, breakfast buffet 32€ (or may come with room depending on rate-type). All major CCs accepted. **Note:** Hotel Sacher Salzburg is the sister property of Hotel Sacher Vienna. Did you know, since 1832, as per a closely guarded secret recipe, Franz Sacher and family have been whipping up the world's most **famous torte:** a rich chocolate cake with a hint of apricot. The 4-portion *Piccolo* size cake presented in a classic-style wooden box with Sacher imprint is a sweet gift idea (21.90€, maximum freshness within 14 days of purchase). To order your Original Sacher Torte, show up in person (café or gift shop) or go to the hotel's website. GPS: N47 48.135 E13 02.565. **Drivers**, a doorman awaits your arrival, parking roughly 35€/day. **Railers**, from the main train station, a taxi will cost around 8€. **From Salzburg airport** a taxi will cost roughly 13€ (depending on traffic; tell the driver you want to be driven through the city [the alternative route is longer via the autobahn]).

$$$$ **Hotel Schloss Mönchstein,** (Mönchsberg Park 26, www.monchstein.at, tel. 0662/848-5550, **free Wi-Fi** and use of Internet computer). "Enchanting" is the first word that comes to mind when considering Schloss Mönchstein, a luxurious 5-star castle hotel perched upon the bluff rising above Salzburg Old Town. Needless to say, the views from here are stupendous! The property, secluded by 4 acres of private forested reserve, was first mentioned in the year 1350 as Tetelheimer Tower. In the coming centuries, aristocrats and prominent persons caught wind of the beloved castle estate and became regular visitors. Today, valued guests are treated to welcome drinks and rooms furnished with precious antiques and contemporary comforts, creating a truly exquisite and personal atmosphere. All told, the hotel has 24 exclusively designed rooms and suites, an award-winning restaurant, a romantic wedding chapel, and a restorative health spa (in which many treatments are available, including an aroma-relax massage 105€/70 min and body peel 48€/30 min). Recent renovations make Hotel Schloss Mönchstein one

of Salzburg's finest choices for accommodations. **PRICE** (includes exclusive a-la-carte breakfast with buffet), Sgl (deduct 20% from the following room categories to get Sgl rate), Dbl 350-650€, Junior suite 695-840€, Schloss suite 795-920€, Maria Theresia suite 1,495-1,600€, Royal suite 1,695-1,900€, extra bed 80€ (6-11yr 40€, 0-5yr free). All major CCs accepted. **Note:** Once settled into the hotel, your means of connecting the Old Town will be on foot (pleasant 25-min walk down) or quicker via the nearby Mönchsberg Lift (page 31). GPS: N47 48.192 E13 02.151. **Drivers**, (enter Müllner Hauptstrasse 10 into your GPS navigation system), free parking on property—the only way up the bluff is via the district of Mülln, home of the Augustinian brewery and monastery (marked by the copper-topped church steeple)—see hotel Web site for print-friendly directions (pdf file). **Railers**, from the main train station, a taxi will cost around 9€ (depending on traffic). **From Salzburg airport** a taxi will cost about 15€ (depending on traffic).

Accommodations better suited for Drivers

$$ (hostel-hotel) **JUFA** listed on page 53 also works well for Drivers since it has a small parking lot (5€/day) out front and is within easy walking distance of the Old Town.

$$ Gästehaus Bonauerhof, (Kapellenweg 5, Viehhausen, , tel. 0662/853-361, www.bonauerhof.at, **free Wi-Fi** and use of Internet computer). I adore these digs, and I think you'll find 'em adorable too. If you're looking for a quiet bed on a working farm in the 'burbs bursting with fresh country air and vast pastoral vistas, this is for you. Gästehaus Bonauerhof is a family run farmhouse by the Götzinger clan, who offer seven reasonably sized apartment-like rooms, each with its own balcony, and big hospitality typically associated with country  folk. Located in the village of Viehhausen, 7 km west of Salzburg Old Town, the Götzingers have plenty of room for you and their stable of horses, dairy cows, and handful of rabbits: Fredi, Tom, Peter and Fani, all whom the children love. Aside from the petting zoo, go for a dip in the natural, spring-fed pool or you're welcome to borrow the family bikes to cycle through the pretty pastures. Your first stop can be the charming chapel across the street to view the historic scene (left of its front door) depicting the raging infernos that swept through the village in 1874. Right of the chapel door is a memorial to the locals who fell during both world wars. **PRICE** (does not include breakfast), cash only; Dbl 70€, Trpl 90€, family (up to 4 pers.) 120€. Book early! There are only 7 rooms. **Note:** Minimum 3 nights required to stay. Consider buying the Salzburg Card (page 9) to save on the sights as well as bus fare to/fro the Old Town. Bus 27 regularly shuttles between Viehhausen and Salzburg Old Town (Hanuschplatz) every day until last bus around 23:00. GPS: N47 46.985 E12 59.252. **Railers**, from the main train station, hop on bus 27 direction Airport and get off at Viehhausen Ortsmitte (30-min ride; either notify driver of your intended stop or push button on handrail to signal driver to stop; bus departs Mon-Fri every 15 min until about 19:59, Sat until 18:32—outside of these hours including Sunday, bus 27 departs Hanuschplatz in the Old Town every 20-30 min until last bus at 23:10). From Viehhausen Ortsmitte it's a short walk; exit bus left then ahead go right at the chapel into (lane) Kapellenweg to your digs on the left. **From Salzburg airport**, a taxi will cost roughly 7€, or ride bus 27 direction Hauptbahnhof and get off at

Viehhausen Ortsmitte (5-min ride; either notify driver of your intended stop or push button on handrail to signal driver to stop; bus departs every 15 min, and every 20-30 min after 19:00 Mon-Sat and all day Sun until last bus at 23:05). From Viehhausen Ortsmitte it's a short walk; exit bus right then go right around the corner and ahead go right at the chapel into (lane) Kapellenweg to your digs on the left. **Drivers**, Gästehaus Bonauerhof is just off the A1 autobahn at exit "Salzburg West." **If you've** just connected onto the A1 from the A10 or Germany, after exiting at Salzburg West turn right toward Salzburg and immediately right again at the Viehhausen sign. Take this road a few hundred meters then turn left at the chapel; this is Kapellenweg and your digs are on the left. **If you're** coming from the east on the A1 (e.g. from Linz or Vienna), after exiting at Salzburg West go all the way around the turning circle direction Salzburg, then ahead (just after the Himmelreich sign) turn right at the Viehhausen sign. Take this road a few hundred meters then turn left at the chapel; this is Kapellenweg and your digs are on the left.

$$ **Motel One (Mirabell)** listed on page 54 also works well for Drivers since it has in-house parking (12€/day) and is within a pleasant walk of the Old Town.

$$ **Star Inn Zentrum,** (Hildmannplatz 5, www.starinnhotels.com, tel. 0662/ 846-846, **free Wi-Fi** and use of Internet computer in lobby). These 3-star economy digs with few frills but modern design and flat-screen TVs add 86 air-conditioned rooms (48 standard, 17 business, 17 family, 4 suites) to Salzburg's accommodations pool for both Railers and Drivers. Conveniently positioned just outside the west end of the Old Town, in front of the Siegmundstor (gate) cutting through the Mönchsberg (Monks' Ridge) to the festival halls and main shopping street, Star Inn's proximity to Mozart's birthplace and other major attractions is just the proverbial cow chip chuck away. **PRICE** (add 10€ to standard and biz rate if you'd like a balcony), standard Sgl from 74€ (biz from 94€, suite from 114€); standard Dbl from 94€ (biz from 114€, suite from 134€); Trpl/family two-dbl beds from 124€ (suite from 154€); quad/family two-dbl beds from 134€ (suite from 164€); breakfast buffet 13€/person. All major CCs accepted. **Note:** Two children up to the age of 11 accompanied by their parents stay for free, including breakfast (if parents booked their own). During the 45-day Salzburg Festival mid-July thru August and Advent, add 60€ per night to the room price. GPS: N47 47.855 E13 02.264. **Drivers**, parking 16€/24hr; exit the A1 autobahn at "Flughafen" and follow signs to Salzburg, then Mitte and Hotel route. After about 4 km you will reach a giant cliff face and a tunnel funneling into the Old Town—don't drive through the tunnel! Before it, on the right, are your digs. Park by hotel and unload. Have reception explain parking situation, including hotel discount. **Railers**, from the main train station, a taxi will cost around 10€, or hop on bus 1 direction Zentrum (departs every 10 min, and every 20 min after 19:00 Mon-Sat and all day Sun) and get off at Reichenhaller Strasse (15-min ride; when the bus goes through the tunnel, Reichenhaller Strasse is the next stop. Push button on handrail to signal driver to stop). Exit bus right, stroll back to the crosswalk and your digs are across the street. **From Salzburg airport**, a taxi will cost around 9€, or ride bus 10 toward town (departing every 15 min, every 30 min after 19:00 Mon-Sat and all day Sun) and get off at Reichenhaller Strasse and your digs (10-min ride). Other than bus 10, another option would be to catch bus 2 outside the airport then connect onto bus 1, like so: ride bus 2 toward town (departing every 10-20 min until about 22:55) and get off a few stops later at Hans-Schmid-Platz (mention this to bus driver upon boarding). From here cross over to bus 1 direction Messe/Arena and get off after a handful of stops at Reichenhaller Strasse and your digs.

$$$ Bergland Hotel, (Rupertgasse 15, www.berglandhotel.at, tel. 0662/872-318, **free Wi-Fi** in lobby, use of Internet computer for purchase). These well-appointed digs secreted behind an unremarkable facade at the top of the New Town, 15 minutes by foot from the Old Town, are a great choice for Drivers who can park out front for free. The owners, Peter and Inga (pictured), a convivial husband-and-wife team, whose family has

been the innkeepers for more than 100 years (since 1912), affectionately run the non-smoking Bergland Hotel and make overnighting in Salzburg a homey experience in a friendly, urban neighborhood. An elevator lifts guests to the upper floors, filled with individually decorated rooms, from traditional to minimalist. Upstairs is a restful terrace, an ideal place to conclude a dreamy day of sightseeing in Salzburg, with a glass of wine in hand. Musically inclined guests chill in the cozy confines of the music room (adjacent to reception) and play piano or strum guitar. In the evening, local cuisine and entertainment begin just a few doors along at Die Weisse (page 42) or down Linzergasse to a smorgasbord of choices. **PRICE** (includes breakfast buffet), Sgl 60-80€, medium Dbl 70-130€, large Dbl 80-150€, Trpl 100-180€, suite (2/3 pers.) 120-210€. CC: VC, MC, AE. **Note:** Add 1.10€ per person per night to price for bed tax. Check-in from 13:00, check-out by 11:00. Reception 7:00-21:30, thus notify reception if checking in late. Salzburg Card sold at reception. **Drivers**, free parking, enter Rupertgasse 15 into your GPS navigation system. **Railers**, from the main train station, a taxi will cost around 8€, or hop on bus 2 direction Zentrum/Obergnigl and get off at Bayerhamerstrasse (6th stop but push button on handrail to signal driver to stop; bus departs every 10 min, and every 20 min after 19:00 Mon-Sat and all day Sun). Exit bus left then go right into lane just past gas station—at end of lane are your digs (left). **From Salzburg airport**, a taxi will cost around 15€ (tell the driver you want to be driven through the city [the alternative route is longer via the autobahn]), or hop on bus 2 toward town and get off at Bayerhamerstrasse, 30-min ride (6th stop after main train station but push button on handrail to signal driver to stop; bus departs every 10 min, and every 20 min after 19:00 Mon-Sat and all day Sun). Exit bus left then go right into lane just past gas station—at end of lane are your digs (left).

$$$ Hotel Untersberg, (Dr. Friedrich Ödlweg 1, St. Leonhard, tel. 06246/72575, www.hoteluntersberg.at, **free Wi-Fi** and use of Internet computer). More bucolic bliss can be found here at Hotel Untersberg, a 4-star rustic retreat with a bona fide Austrian feel idyllically nestled at the foot of Untersberg mountain, on the road connecting Salzburg with Berchtesgaden, 13 km (or 8 mi) to either destination. Country-style furnishings accent spacious rooms that fill with fresh alpine air puffing in from scenic summer balconies dripping with vibrant geraniums while every half hour a cable car ascends to the summit of Untersberg mountain (page 35, see reception for your cable-car discount as well as free use of a bicycle for pedaling around the edelweiss). **PRICE** (includes breakfast buffet and use of sauna), Sgl (Salzburg Land) 73€/*80€, Sgl (Kaiser Karl) 85€/*93€, Dbl (Salzburg Land) 123€/*137€, Dbl (Kaiser Karl) 139€/*153€, Trpl and apartment available, (*high season: Aug-Sept, Advent weekends, and Dec 21 thru Jan 2). All major CCs accepted. **Note:** Hotel Untersberg groups its rooms into two comfort categories: the Salzburg Land and Kaiser Karl. Although both are fine, choose the superior Kaiser Karl category which is situated in the main building. Sauna open 16:30-21:00—ask reception for bathrobe. For your dining pleasure, Hotel Untersberg has a traditional Austrian restaurant seeking to indulge your palate. Consider buying the Salzburg Card (page 9) from reception to save on the sights as well as bus fare to/fro the Old Town. GPS: N47 43.612 E13 02.597. **Railers**, I don't recommend this hotel for you because of its distance from the Old Town, but just in case you need the directions: from the main train station hop on bus 25 direction Untersbergbahn (departing every 20 min, and every 30 min after 18:00 Mon-Fri and 17:00 Sat/Sun) and ride it to the end, 30 min. **Drivers**, free parking on property; exit A10 autobahn at Salzburg-Süd and head toward Grödig—after 1 km you'll see the hotel's (flowering) facade on the right (turn at traffic light). After you've checked in and are ready to head into Salzburg, either catch bus 25 (departing every 20-30 min from behind hotel) or drive into town and park (see Drivers/Parking page 8).

$$$ Hotel-Garni Scherrthaler & Gasthof zur Post: Although a fair distance from Salzburg, 27 km to be specific, I've listed these two digs here because if you're heading out to the lake district (Salzkammergut page 69) and are open to spending the night in a lakeside village, then consider either accommodations (pages 73-74) located on the tremendously scenic Wolfgangsee.

$$$ Trapp Villa, (Traunstrasse 34, Aigen, 3 km southeast of Old Town, tel. 0662/630-860, www.villa-trapp.com, free Wi-Fi in foyer, book in advance via an online wholesaler for best rate). At the Trapp Villa you have the opportunity to overnight in the former residence of Salzburg's most famous family, page 99.

Camping:

Panorama, (Rauchenbichler Strasse 21, GPS: N47 49.726 E13 03.154, open mid-March thru Oct and over the New Year holidays, office generally 8:00-23:00, check-out by 12:00, www.panorama-camping.at, tel. 0662/450-652). Living up to its name, Camping Panorama (having some 70 tent/RV sites) is parked on a restful ridge set before stunning views that stretch across Salzburg. Moreover, it has all the necessities a camper would desire, including laundry facilities (washer-dryer), a bistro with sun terrace (mid-May thru Sept), and apartment-style living for 2-5 people who prefer the comforts of home. Camping price varies depending on configuration and season; for example, space for a car and tent is 10€, then 10€ per adult per night (thus two people with a tent and car would cost 30€ per night). Camping Panorama is positioned 3 km north of the Old Town. **Drivers**, exit A1 autobahn at "Salzburg Nord" direction Salzburg and immediately follow camping (Stadtblick) signs right up the hill.

Schloss Aigen, (located on the lane Weberbartlweg but enter "Glaserstrasse" into your navigation system, open May-Sept, office generally 7:30-22:45, cash only, www.campingaigen.com, tel. 0662/622-079). Campground Aigen is situated 5 km southeast of the Old Town in a leafy, rural area that epitomizes tranquility—even the drive here is wunderbar! Moreover, the distant views across green meadows to the fortress are mesmeric. The 120-site campground also affords its guests an on-site beer garden and casual restaurant (that milk, butter, bread, and Würst for grilling can also be purchased 7:00-22:00). Camping price varies depending on configuration; for example, space for a car and tent is 6€, then 8€ per adult per night, youth 4-15yr 3.50€ (thus two adults with a tent and car would cost 22€ per night). GPS: N47 46.791 E13 05.470. **Drivers**, exit A10 autobahn at Salzburg-Süd and drive towards Salzburg. After about 4 km turn right (immediately past the Park+Ride) direction Aigen. Continue straight and cross the river. Go around and left on the upcoming traffic circle, then make the second right following the camping signs all the way through the residential area. Immediately after the petite bridge over the babbling brook, turn right. **SOM fans**, you're near the real von Trapp villa (page 99).

EXCURSIONS

Salzkammergut, (page 69): 15 km east of Salzburg begins this breathtakingly beautiful lake district.

Berchtesgaden, (see my "Self-guided Berchtesgaden & Hitler's Eagle's Nest" guide). Some 25 km southwest of Salzburg (on the German side of the border) is Berchtesgaden, a quiet Bavarian village nestled amongst the edelweiss-encrusted Alps. Here you'll find the Eagle's Nest, salt mines, and Königssee lake. To get there from Salzburg is easy, see page 7 (Getting to Berchtesgaden). Or, if interested, pricey tours are available to Berchtesgaden from Salzburg; ask TI or staff at your digs for info.

Mauthausen: Consider visiting Austria's former notorious concentration camp— now an affecting memorial—on the way to Vienna. **Railers**, have the railway clerk from your point of departure print out an itinerary (Fahrplanauskunft) to the town of Mauthausen (OÖ) and then back again from Mauthausen to St. Valentin to connect with the Salzburg-Vienna rail line. **Drivers**, Mauthausen is about 150 km northeast of Salzburg via the A1 autobahn direction Vienna; get off at exit 151, St. Valentin, then follow signs to Mauthausen and KZ "Memorial."

☞ Similar to the Bayern-Ticket in Bavaria, the **Einfach-Raus-Ticket** is a terrific buy in Austria for small groups (up to five persons) traveling on non-speed trains for the day in 2nd-class seating on the Austrian rail network: ÖBB. The price for two to five persons (irrespective of age) is **36€**, valid Mon-Fri 9:00 until 3:00 (the following morning) and the whole day Sat/Sun on ÖBB's suburban and regional service trains as well as on the Raaberbahn (R, REX and S-Bahn). **This group ticket would be ideal**, for example, for a day trip from Salzburg to Werfen (page 66) or Hallstatt (page 75), or five persons to Oberndorf (below). **Note:** Unlike the Bayern-Ticket, the Einfach-Raus-Ticket is not valid on buses or the subway, only suburban and regional ÖBB trains. Einfach-Raus-Tickets are available for purchase online (www.oebb.at), at ÖBB automats, or over the counter at the train station.

Oberndorf bei Salzburg

Population: 5,995. **Elevation:** 394 m (1,292 ft). **Country-Area code:** +43-(0)6272.
License plate: SL (short for Salzburgland, the rural district around Salzburg).

Some 22 km north of Salzburg is Oberndorf, a cute border town huddled on the Austrian side of the Salzach River (on the opposite bank is its medieval twin: Laufen, Germany). Oberndorf flourished through the ages as a key partner along a trade route flushed with merchant vessels hauling salt, regarded then as "white gold." Although Oberndorf has a rich history dating from the 12th century, it is a single incident that transpired over the course of just a few minutes that forever labeled the riverside community as an international tourist destination. On Christmas Eve, 1818, Joseph Mohr (the village priest) required a carol to accompany midnight Mass at St. Nicholas' church. Mohr handed Franz Xaver Gruber (school teacher and part-time organist) a poem that he had written and asked him to compose a simple melody befitting the text. Gruber finished the melody in time for midnight Mass and the two men, along with the choir, sang the newly composed carol to a delighted crowd. The carol was called *Stille Nacht,* or more famously, "Silent Night."

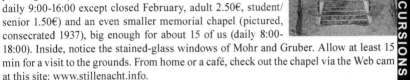

Throughout history, communities were preferably settled on the banks of rivers as a means to a robust trading economy. A geographic location such as this, however, could also spell disaster! You see, in the year 1890, Mother Nature dialed up a devastating flood, in which the Salzach River overflowed its banks and St. Nicholas' church standing in the path was irreversibly damaged. Today, the former church grounds on Stille Nacht Platz consist only of the small "Heimat" museum (explaining history of town, salt merchants, and Silent Night story, daily 9:00-16:00 except closed February, adult 2.50€, student/senior 1.50€) and an even smaller memorial chapel (pictured, consecrated 1937), big enough for about 15 of us (daily 8:00-18:00). Inside, notice the stained-glass windows of Mohr and Gruber. Allow at least 15 min for a visit to the grounds. From home or a café, check out the chapel via the Web cam at this site: www.stillenacht.info.

EXCURSIONS

Every year on December 24, tour buses usher in hundreds of tourists to join locals in a Silent Night memorial service, when hot-spiced wine (Glühwein) is sipped from collector's mugs, traditional Christmas shooters chase away evil spirits, and joyous revelers sing the world-renowned carol. The memorial service begins at 17:00 and lasts about 45 minutes (but plan to arrive by 16:15 to allow for people and car traffic). During the weeks leading up to Christmas, the Silent Night Post Office will be open for business (daily from about December 8 thru Christmas Eve, located in the "Heimat" museum, where souvenirs are also sold and information given). Bring in your letters and postcards to be mailed and the clerk will strike them with a specially designed "Silent Night" postmark.

GPS: N47 56.736 E12 56.200. **Railers,** from Salzburg's central station, trains depart for Oberndorf (bei Salzburg) typically every 30 min at the top and bottom of the hour (25-min trip, www.svv-info.at). From Oberndorf train station, it's a 10-min walk to the memorial chapel. (Note the train departure times so you can neatly plan your return to Salzburg.) Exit station left and at the main road go right. Cross the street at the upcoming crosswalk and continue in the same direction along the main road. After about 600 meters follow the Stille Nacht Kapelle sign left and the chapel will appear on the right. **Drivers,** the scenic drive from Salzburg to Oberndorf is roughly 30 min. Take route 20 on the German side of the border. To find it, head to Freilassing in northwest Salzburg. After crossing the border you'll meet route 20; follow signs to Laufen, 13 km. Once in Laufen follow signs to Oberndorf, which will lead through the town's medieval gate (circa 1400) and narrow streets. Soon you'll cross the Salt River (Salzach)—halfway across the turn-of-the-century iron bridge is Austria—the other side is Oberndorf. (In June 2003, both

Germany and Austria commemorated this striking Art Nouveau-style bridge on a postage stamp to mark its 100th birthday. Pictured is the stamp from Germany.) If it's a clear day, notice the sweeping vista of the Alps to your right. Continue straight towards the church in front of you; at the T-intersection, turn left. After 1 km look for a parking space (preferably on the right curve). The chapel (Stille Nacht Kapelle) is accessible via a footpath on the left (just prior to right curve). If there are no parking spaces available, turn left into the lane at Gasthof Bauernbräu for more options. When heading back to Salzburg, take route 156 on the Austrian side. This is the main road running through Oberndorf, which southbound will land you in Salzburg (16 km).

Werfen

Population: 3,000. **Elevation:** 547 m (1,794 ft). **Country-Area code:** +43-(0)6468.
License plate: JO (short for Sankt Johann, district of Pongau, to which Werfen belongs)

When heading south from Salzburg you'll encounter massive, sheer mountains flanking your journey—an overwhelming spectacle, indeed. Among this chain of Alps is the town of Werfen, 40 km south of Salzburg. Most of the time it's hard to distinguish one village from another in this region since they all feature an idyllic church steeple soaring above a cluster of well-kept houses accentuated by colorful flowers spilling over their balconies. However, there is one thing that differentiates Werfen from neighboring communities, and that is one hunka-chunka castle: Burg Hohenwerfen, kid brother to the Salzburg fortress. It is truly an awesome sight to behold this medieval citadel perched above Werfen, defining its skyline. Moreover, Werfen possesses the world's largest ice cave. In addition, classic moviegoers will be interested to know that Werfen appeared in "The Sound of Music," and in a much bigger role it was the town portrayed in the 1968 movie "Where Eagles Dare" starring Clint Eastwood and Richard Burton. (In German, the film was called *Agenten sterben einsam*, meaning "agents die alone.") And so, when you marvel this tremendous scenery in person and envision its natural beauty to be right out of a Hollywood movie, you can be certain that it is.

Suggestion: If you're planning on doing both the ice cave and castle, do the ice cave first then the castle second to avoid crowds on, and in, the mountain (especially July/ Aug). To save time, in the shuttle bus back down from the ice cave, have the driver drop you off at the trailhead to the castle (Burg Hohenwerfen). **Railers**, from Salzburg's central station, trains depart hourly for Werfen (40-min trip, www.svv-info.at). From Werfen train station, you can pick up the shuttle to the ice cave (for times see Ice Cave below), or mosey 10 min into town to the TI (cross bridge over river and continue straight), or march 30 min to the castle (cross bridge over river and go right along riverside path following signs to fortress). **Drivers**, Werfen is a 30-min drive from Salzburg via the A10 autobahn south, direction Graz-Villach. You are allowed to park on the main drag cutting through the center of town for one hour free with your parking dial (page 102) during the hours Mon-Fri 8:00-18:00, Sat 8:00-12:00; all other times the dial is not required.

Tourist information (generally Mon-Fri 9:00-12:30 & 13:00-18:00, November open only Tue-Wed, www.werfen.at, tel. 06468/5388) is located at Markt 24, on the main drag in the center of town, within a 10-min walk of the train station. Friendly staff can assist you with any local questions or finding accommodations.

The **post office** (Mon-Fri 7:00-12:00 & 14:30-18:00, Sat 7:00-12:00) is located within the magazine shop Nadegger at Markt 41, roughly 200 meters down from the TI (towards train station).

A **pharmacy** (Mon-Fri 8:00-12:00 & 14:30-18:00, Sat 8:00-12:00), locally Apotheke, is situated at Markt 23, across the street from the above-listed tourist information office.

Remember, in Austria, even if it's just plain aspirin you require, it can only be purchased at an Apotheke (this goes the same for Germany).

An "Mpreis" **mini mart** (grocery store, Mon-Fri 8:00-18:30, Sat 8:00-17:00) is positioned a few doors along from the above-listed tourist information office.

Burg Hohenwerfen, www.salzburg-burgen.at, open April 1 thru Oct 31, 2015: April (Monday closed) and Oct 9:30-16:00 (except closed Oct 19); May-Sept 9:00-17:00; July 20 thru Aug 14, 9:00-18:00. Price (includes birds-of-prey show, weapons exhibition, museum, and the castle tour departing most every hour on the hour, 20% off with valid Salzburg Card), adult 11€ (with railway 14.50€), student 9.50€ (with railway 12.50€), youth 6-15yr 6€ (with railway 8€), family 26.50€ (with railway 34.50€). Allow at least two hours for a visit. Time your arrival to coincide with the birds-of-prey show (flight demonstrations daily 11:15 and 15:15, except July 21 thru Aug 15 at 11:15, 14:15 and 16:30), duration 30 min.

©Werfen Tourism

EXCURSIONS

Dating from 1077 A.D., this imposing castle rests upon a forested bluff towering over the village of Werfen. Its powerful bulwarks firmly entrenched into the rock-solid earth persuasively served throughout the Middle Ages to imprison high-value convicts as well as further protect the trade route connecting Italy. Today, the citadel stands as a footprint of history alongside a sleek autobahn delivering adventurers and moneyed tourists who keenly pay admission to marvel the castle's medieval matrix and mesmerizing birds-of-prey show. **Note:** To avoid the 15-min hike up to the fortress, take the **cable railway** directly from the castle parking lot (see Drivers below) lifting straight into the fortifications. **Special programs** for big and little kids alike are fun, fascinating and held frequently at the fortress, thus I've listed the following dates and happenings to help you plan your Werfen visit. I recommend the "Mittelalterliches Treiben auf der Burg," or medieval festival with jugglers and fencing in period dress and knights' tournament for children, scheduled in 2015 from 10:00-17:00 May 24-25, June 13-14, July 4-5, and Sept 5-6 & 26-27. **To get there**, the fortress can only be reached on foot or by cable railway; there is no shuttle service. If you're without wheels and can't be bothered walking, call **Taxi Seiwald** (tel. 06468/5381) to take you to the castle parking lot to connect with the cable railway (note there is no taxi stand at the train station therefore call Seiwald in advance to schedule your pick-up, otherwise you may have to wait a short while for him to arrive from a neighboring village). **Railers**, at your point of departure, small groups consider purchasing the "Einfach-Raus-Ticket" (page 64, from Salzburg, catch the 9:08 train). Once at Werfen train station, you can reach the fortress either via taxi (see Taxi Seiwald) to the cable railway or on foot (roughly a 30-min trek, cross bridge over river and go right along riverside path following signs to the fortress; first flat, then steep). **Drivers**, Werfen is a 30-min drive from Salzburg via the A10 autobahn south, direction Graz-Villach, (Vignette required, page 102). The castle parking lot (<u>GPS</u>: N47 28.983 E13 11.121, free parking, toilets) is located below the fortress on route 159. From the A10 autobahn south, get off at the exit "Pass-Lueg" and drive route 159 south a handful of kilometers to the castle parking lot, found a short distance after the village of Tenneck. From the lot, you can either hike up to the fortress (15 min) or if foot-weary hop on the new cable railway lifting straight into the castle grounds.

SOM fans, you'll see the abovementioned fortress (Burg Hohenwerfen) in the movie "The Sound of Music." Forward to the scene where Maria and the kids are playing in a grassy meadow while wearing their play clothes and learning to sing "Do-Re-Mi." The significant structure in the background is Werfen's castle, and the meadow they are in is called Gschwandtanger. I recommend a visit here if you've got time—plan your stop around midday to complement the dreamy views with a picnic. To find Gschwandtanger will either be quite easy or somewhat tiring, depending on your mode of transportation. GPS: N47 28.413 E13 10.847. **Railers,** stop by the TI; staff will give you a map and point the way up Poststraße and through the woods (steep, 30 min). **Drivers,** follow the above set of directions I've written for Drivers heading to Burg Hohenwerfen, but pass the castle parking lot and turn right off route 159 toward Gasthof Dielalm. Climb the frightfully narrow, two-way zigzagging road a little more than one kilometer. Once on the other side of the forest, the view will become familiar—on the left is the SOM meadow. Continue driving and soon you'll see two benches ahead beneath a cluster of maple trees—just beyond them, before the curve, is a good place to pull over. **Picnickers,** in Werfen, pick up your goodies at the "Mpreis" mini mart (see its entry above) and/or the deli at Markt 36 (when facing the TI, go left several doors to the flowering facade of the Fleischhauerei). **Note:** When absorbing the views on Gschwandtanger, look above the castle about three-fourths of the way up the mountain. Now move your eyes left and you'll see a white structure; this belongs to the ice cave (next entry). If you have a fear of heights, scratch this attraction off your list of things to do.

Ice Cave, locally Eisriesenwelt, (www.eisriesenwelt.at, open May thru October 26, cashier daily May-June & Sept-Oct 8:00-15:00 but last cable car at 15:20, July-Aug cashier till 16:00 but last cable car at 16:20; **price** includes cable car and guided cave tour: 22€, student 20€, youth 15-18yr 16€, child 5-14yr 12€, family 31€[1+1]-62€[2+2], without cable car 6-11€ but it's about a 90-min hike; **tour** duration 75 min; overall, expect a visit to take between 3 and 4 hours; if interested, commercial tours are available to the ice cave from Salzburg, ask TI or staff at your digs).

For a chilling experience, visit the world's largest ice cave concealed within the Tennen Alp range—more than 40 km of caverns have been explored! The giant ice cave, discovered by a wandering naturalist in 1879, is located at a dizzying height upon the mountain opposite Burg Hohenwerfen (other side of autobahn). Today, it is a nationally protected landmark and may only be entered with a guide. To reach the mouth of the cave is serious business, not for the faint hearted. First, either by car or shuttle bus, travelers must climb the mega-steep (21% grade) 5 km mountain road to arrive at the parking lot. From here, it's a 20-min walk uphill to the cable car—Austria's steepest cable-car ascent, 500 m (1,640 ft) in 3 minutes—which will lift a dozen passengers (many of whom will see God in the vertical mountain face on the way up) to the elevation of 1,575 m (5,166 ft). The vista, needless to say, is phenomenal! From here, one teeters high above the valley floor while trekking another 20 minutes to reach the mouth of the cave. At this point, many adventurers will be sweating from head to toe, but it is essential to throw on a jacket or sweater, or both. Once the entrance to the cave is exposed, bystanders will be belted by an arctic blast as if being hurled into a giant freezer. *Burrr.* Inside is pitch black, except for the light emanating from the lamps provided by the guide—a surreal environment of ice, rock, and darkness. **Note:** Travelers who are out of shape, have a fear of heights, or suffer from vertigo—save your money and delete this attraction from your itinerary. Travelers who are in good health and have a sense of adventure should find the time and money to experience the world's largest ice cave. Wear good hiking shoes and pack warm clothes (because the temps inside the cave are literally freezing, 0°C/32°F,

EXCURSIONS

year round)! Adjacent to the upper cable-car station, a scenic chalet-style restaurant is keen to serve you. Views are paralyzing! Photography inside cave is *verboten!* (That said, your guide might not enforce it.) The **shuttle bus** to the ice cave (6.50€/adult) departs Werfen regularly, about every 25 min, from the big parking area along the riverbank, a 5-min walk from the train station. **Railers,** from outside Werfen's train station the shuttle bus to the ice cave (6.50€/adult) departs 8:18, 10:18, 12:18 and 14:18 (if you missed the shuttle then cross the bridge, go right and follow the riverside path for about 5 min to the big parking area where the shuttle departs every 25 min), or it's possible to **hike up to the cable car** departure area (6 km, steep) taking around two hours. **Drivers,** follow signs Eisriesenwelt. Slip car into first gear and admire the views *after* parking.

Salzkammergut

This strange-sounding name translates to "salt storage estates," referring to the region's rich salt deposits that have been mined since the Iron Age, i.e. Hallstatt. Today, however, the Salzkammergut (www.salzkammergut.at) is better known as the lake district—a collection of glacial lakes strung out like shimmering pearls across three Austrian states: Salzburgland, Styria (Steiermark), and Upper Austria (Oberösterreich). Besides its stunning beauty, another exclusive feature of the Salzkammergut is that many of the alpine lakes boast crystal-clear drinking-quality water. It's pure!

Within reach of Salzburg, the main lakes of interest are Fuschlsee, Wolfgangsee, Mondsee and Hallstätter See, hence this Salzkammergut section focuses on these destinations. While reviewing the aforesaid names, you'll notice they all have one thing in common: the suffix "see," which in German (pronounced 'zay') means "lake."

Sound of Music fans will be interested to know that a few scenes from the movie were filmed in this region, principally the wedding scene at Mondsee (pages 75 & 98).

Suggestion: If it's a warm day, bring your bathing suit and pack a picnic. Those of you who are planning on spending the night, choose between Wolfgangsee and Hallstätter See—either destination is stunning. **Note:** To obtain a discount on most every attraction mentioned in this chapter, including public transportation, purchase the **Salzkammergut Erlebnis Card** (adult 3.90€-4.90€, valid May thru Oct for the duration of your stay, available at most any TI/info stand and hotel in the Salzkammergut).

Fuschlsee

Situated 15 km east of Salzburg, Fuschlsee is the first lake you'll come to after leaving the city limits. Its glistening turquoise-colored waters, warming up to a pleasant 24-degrees Celsius (75°F) in summer, allure even the most hardcore urbanites. Drivers and their passengers will parallel the four-kilometer-long Lake Fuschl before reaching the main village upon its shores, aptly named **Fuschl am See**. Although petite, Fuschl am See commands a devout loyalty from vacationers who return annually with their campers and tents to claim a sliver of shoreline for yet another sizzling season on one of the warmest lakes in the Salzkammergut.

In contrast to the pocket-friendly joys of camping are the ultra-exclusive digs of **Schloss Fuschl**, a 15th-century estate recently converted into one of Austria's leading resort hotels (that is largely out of view from passing motorists). Originally built in 1450 for the archbishop as a summer hideaway and hunting lodge, Schloss Fuschl (Schloss

LAKE DISTRICT

Strasse 19, Hof bei Salzburg, www.schlossfuschlresort.com, tel. 06229/22530) is idylli-cally snuggled on the water's edge, surrounded by a 35-acre nature reserve. To get there, turn at the Hotel Jagdhof, located on the west (Salzburg) side of Lake Fuschl, just after the town of Hof. WWII buffs will be interested to know that Joachim von Ribbontrop, Hitler's foreign minister, acquired Schloss Fuschl in 1938 for his holiday home. After the defeat of Nazism, the property became an R&R resort for Allied soldiers until 1950.

As you approach (the town) Fuschl am See, on the right you'll see a number of build-ings, among them a pair of saucer-shaped structures standing like dormant volcanoes

rising from a man-made lagoon (pictured) that pin-points the world headquarters of the caffeine-rich en-ergy drink and billion-dollar brand, **Red Bull**. The company's founder, local-resident Dietrich Mate-schitz, is a marketing mastermind, who proposed to sell an unknown and overpriced product for which there was no existing market, then successfully sold copious amounts of the product to land him on the list of the world's richest people. Remarkable! In 1984, 40-year-old Mateschitz founded Red Bull in Austria, where it is still exclusively pro-duced. The brand burst onto the German market a decade later, then the world in 1997 (California being the first US market that year). Today, Red Bull (www.redbull.com) is a multibillion-dollar company, having more than 10,000 employees in 167 countries, in-cluding Austria where it is the nation's most profitable single brand. To view Mateschitz's collection of vintage aircraft, swing by Hangar-7 (page 34) in Salzburg.

Immediately following Red Bull is a sign pointing to the Sommerrodelbahn (sum-mer toboggan run). If you're into tight curves and thrilling adventure, skip this 600-me-ter-long (1,968 ft) toboggan and head to the much bigger 1,300-meter (4,264 ft) track at the next lake, Wolfgangsee.

Wolfgangsee

This area is so stunningly beauti-ful that anyone who is planning to travel throughout Austria should adhere to the old adage: "Save the best for last." Those who come here first will dream of the delight-ful shores of Lake Wolfgang for the remainder of their journey—even Austria's Romantic Road meanders past Wolfgangsee to include its splendor. The two main resort towns adorning the lake's shoreline are St. Gilgen and St. Wolfgang. The latter is a storybook village dating from the year 976, when Bishop Wolfgang founded a chapel here. Nestled on the far shore, St. Wolfgang is punctuated by a 213-foot-tall steeple belonging to the town's 15th-century pilgrimage church with museum-like in-terior. Another town attraction is the celebrated but pricey Weissen Rössl (White Horse Inn, since 1878), romantically rooted on the waterfront.

Of the two resort towns, **St. Gilgen** (pop. 3,700, elevation 542m/1,778ft) is by far the most visited by English-speaking travelers since it's closest to Salzburg and it sits at the junction between Fuschlsee, Mondsee and Hallstätter See. What's more, St. Gilgen is the birthplace of Mozart's mother, Anna Maria Walburga Pertl, who is remembered at the Mozart Museum (see next page). And many of you have already seen St. Gilgen (pictured) in the opening of the movie, "The Sound of Music." St. Gilgen was first mentioned in 1376 and takes its name from Saint Giles (locally *der Heilige Ägydius*), whom the parish church is dedicated (you'll see its bulbous tower rising above town).

Wolfgangsee is situated 27 km east of Salzburg, 7 km beyond Fuschlsee and 15 km from Mondsee. The lake is 11 km long, a recreational paradise encircled by a curtain of majestic peaks, and like Fuschlsee it also warms up to an inviting 24-degrees Celsius (75°F) in summer. One of the aforesaid peaks, positioned across from St. Gilgen, is Sheep Mountain (see next page), where a 110-year-old cogwheel train (seen in the movie SOM) lifts tourists to jaw-dropping views. Rising above St. Gilgen, multicolored cable cars quietly ascend to the summit of Zwölferhorn mountain (see next page), where hikers absorb sweeping vistas and adrenaline-pumped junkies paraglide off the edge and soar like hushed eagles. Farther along the mountainous skyline is the super slick toboggan run (see next page) challenging speedsters down the hillside on an aluminum track (1.3 km long) with only a flimsy joystick as a brake. Other area activities include boat rides, swimming, cow tipping, and picnics on alpine meadows.

Tourist information (www.wolfgangsee.at, Mondsee Bundesstr. 1a, St. Gilgen, tel. 06227/2348, Mon-Fri 9:00-17:00, longer hours May-Sept including weekends, e.g. July/Aug Mon-Fri 9:00-19:00, Sat 9:00-18:00, Sun 10:00-17:00) has English-speaking staff, umpteen brochures, and an ATM (but this money machine may incur a significant withdrawal fee). GPS: N47 46.153 E13 21.574. TI is located on the main road (route 158) running along St. Gilgen, adjacent to the Spar grocery store—within a 15-min walk of the ferry dock. **Railers**, the bus stops within a 5-min walk from TI. **Drivers**, when descending into town from Fuschlsee, go right on the traffic circle (direction Bad Ischl) and the TI will appear on the right.

Railers, to get to St. Gilgen from Salzburg catch bus 150 (direction Bad Ischl) from the Hauptbahnhof or Mirabellplatz (hrly, 50-min trip, adult one way 6.50€, day ticket 13€, youth 15-18yr 4.50€/9.10€ and 6-14yr 3.30€/6.60€, www.svv-info.at), or from Mondsee catch bus 156 (20-min trip, adult one way 3.30€, day ticket 6.60€, youth 15-18yr 2.30€/4.50€ and 6-14yr 1.70€/3.40€, but plan ahead because bus departs irregularly, e.g. 3/day Mon-Fri, 1/day Sat, and none on Sun).

Drivers, from north Salzburg, follow signs to St. Gilgen (after crossing railroad tracks on Linzer Bundesstrasse turn right—this road goes to Fuschlsee then Wolfgangsee). If you're coming from **Salzburg** on the A1 autobahn (heading east direction Vienna), take exit No. 274 (Thalgau) and drive towards Hof then Fuschlsee to St. Gilgen. If you're coming from **Vienna** on the A1 autobahn (heading west direction Salzburg), take the Mondsee exit (No. 264) and drive along the lake to St. Gilgen. In St. Gilgen, parking automats by the shore cost (daily 8:00-18:00) 50¢/30 min for a max of 90 min or pay 4€ for all-day parking in one of the two central lots, or free parking (for three hours, daily 8:00-18:00, otherwise unrestricted) can be found in the lot on Sonnburggasse off Aberseestrasse (GPS: N47 45.946 E13 22.001). **Note:** To reach St. Wolfgang is roughly 20 km beyond St. Gilgen; follow signs direction Bad Ischl and at the end of the lake turn left.

Grocery Store: Adjacent to the TI is a Spar grocery store (Mon-Fri 7:00-19:00, Sat 7:00-18:00, Sun 7:30-11:00); another option is Billa (Mon-Fri 7:15-19:30, Sat 7:15-18:00) located above town, on the right when descending into St. Gilgen from Fuschlsee.

Mozart Museum, (located at Ischlerstrasse 15, a brief walk from the ferry dock, open June-Sept Tue-Sun 10:00-12.00 & 15:00-18:00, closed remainder of year, adult 4€, youth 6-18yr 2.50€, allow 25 min for a visit, www.mozarthaus.info). This small memorial museum, known as the "Mozarthaus," features a well-composed *exhibition that remembers Mozart's mother, Anna Maria Walburga Pertl, who was born at this address on Christmas day 1720, but mostly the museum focuses on the life of Mozart's sister, nicknamed "Nannerl," who lived here from 1784-1801. (*Note that few period furnishings exist from Mozart's time and Anna Maria's birth room is upstairs and typically off-limits.) Anna Maria's father (Mozart's grandpa) originally built the house, which doubled as the district courthouse. The fountain outside depicts Anna Maria as a young girl.

Mozart's Square, GPS: N47 46.021 E13 21.851. In the heart of St. Gilgen is Mozartplatz, a picturesque square featuring a statue of Mozart playing violin. Behind him is the three-story Rathaus, or town hall, arguably the most eye-catching building in town, having an adorable bay window and decorative facade. Opposite is the recommended Gasthof zur Post (see Good Sleeps below), where Mozart's sister was married in 1784. When standing in front of and facing Mozart, his right elbow is pointing to Hotel Schafbergspitze at the summit of Sheep Mountain (see next page).

Zwölferhorn, (www.12erhorn.at). Locally known as Erlebnisberg, or "adventure mountain," the Zwölferhorn above St. Gilgen can be scaled in just 16 minutes by riding a colorful cable car to its summit (1,522m/4,993ft). Tourist information has an excellent brochure listing the hiking trails here as well as elevations and details of the surrounding mountains. The cable car (round trip adult 22€, student 20.50€, youth 14.50€, one way 15.50€/15€/10.50€) is open year round daily 9:15-16:00, June-Aug till 18:00, except closed Nov. When you're ready to descend off the summit for the lake, paraglide down. If you're a novice like me, go tandem (120€, tel. 07612/73033, mobile 0664/111-6099, www.paragleiten.net).

Boat Rides, (www.wolfgangseeschifffahrt.at, tel. 06138/22320). A cruise on Wolfgangsee is a summer joy. Hop on a ferry in St. Gilgen (boat dock <u>GPS</u>: N47 45.942 E13 22.082) and ride it to St. Wolfgang, 45 min. Boats depart St. Gilgen: May-Oct every 60-90 min from morning (9:00-10:00) until early evening (18:00), and March-April Sat-Sun 11:55, 14:10 (but note last boat back from St. Wolfgang is 15:30). Round trip from St. Gilgen to St. Wolfgang 14.60€, to Strobl 19.40€ (other end of lake), or purchase an all-day ticket (Tageskarte) adult 19.40€, youth 6-14yr 9.70€, family 39.40€, dog/bike 3.60€. Another way to cruise the lake is to rent an electric boat at the ferry dock (May-Sept, max 5 pax): 14€/30 min, 20€/60 min, 50€/3 hr. Other watercraft available, mobile 0664/585-0891, www.wassersport-engel.at.

Sheep Mountain, locally Schafberg. The Sheep Mountain railway, or Schafbergbahn, as it's called, can be found leisurely climbing the 1,732 m (5,682 ft) high Sheep Mountain, adjacent to St. Wolfgang, across the lake from St. Gilgen. The railway operates on old-timer cogwheels that interlock with the grooved track to prevent slippage. Thus the journey to the summit takes 35 minutes to scale the six-kilometer stretch, which was constructed from 1892-93 by some 350 Italian workers. (SOM fans, there are a pair of cogwheel trains here; one of them is the historic steam train that was briefly shown in the movie during the "Do-Re-Mi" curtain-wearing sequence, and it's possible for you to ride!) Be sure to visit on a good-weather day; from the summit you'll behold spectacular views of pristine lakes, lush meadows and majestic mountains. Catering to the appetite of famished tourists, Sheep Mountain accommodates two restaurants (one is set within Hotel Schafbergspitze, overnight Dbl with breakfast 98€, or package incl. railway 153€, considerable discount when staying a second night, cash only, tel. 06138/3542, www.schafberg.net). The Sheep Mountain railway (www.schafbergbahn.at, tel. 06138/22320) departs April 25 thru Oct 26, 2015 daily, every hour from about 9:15 till 15:00 depending on weather; last train down around 17:00 (but times vary, thus check at summit then reserve your seat down). Price, adult rt 33€, ow 22.70€, family rt (2+1 6-14yr) 74€, combo boat and railway adult 46€, youth 6-14yr 23€—add 10€ to ride the historic **steam train**, locally Dampfzug, departing every Sunday July 5 thru Aug 30, 2015 at 9:25 in good weather (minimum of 20 pax required). The Schafbergbahn railway is reachable via boat from the ferry dock at St. Gilgen (35-min trip), or Drivers follow signs to St. Wolfgang then Schafbergbahn.

Toboggan run (<u>GPS</u>: N47 42.977 E13 26.495), locally Riesenrutschbahnen, meaning "giant sliding chutes," is an exhilarating ride with stupendous views to boot, located directly on route 158, right side (about 10 km) when coming from St. Gilgen. The two tracks here are each 1,300 meters long, that's 4,265 ft, or nearly one mile. After paying admission (one ride adult 7€, youth 5.80€, 10 rides family 49.50€), grab a sled, catch a lift to the top and blaze down the twisting course at a speed you control by the hand throttle. The fun happens, May-Sept 10:00-18:00, July/Aug till 19:00-20:00, but not in bad weather. Call if you're not sure, tel. 06137/7085, www.rodelbahnen.at. If you enjoyed your time here, then you must experience the mother of all Austrian toboggan runs, the 2,200-meter luge at Dürrnberg (page 36), 20 km south of Salzburg. I dare you!

GOOD SLEEPS: The following three digs, listed in order of price, are centrally located in St. Gilgen, come with breakfast, and have a shower/bath and toilet in the room.

$$$ **Gasthof zur Post,** (Mozartplatz 8, www.gasthofzurpost.at, tel. 06227/ 2157, **free Wi-Fi**). Gemütlichkeit at Gasthof zur Post isn't just a term, it's the real deal. Receiving rights to serve beer in 1415, Gasthof zur Post is a historic gem nearly 600 years old! And nobody is more proud of the fact than the owners (since 1999) and your cordial hosts: Katharina and Norbert Leitner. Catching the eye of all who enter, the provincial mural

spanning the front facade dates from 1618 and depicts scenes of noblemen hunting game. The hotel again entered the history books on August 23, 1784, when Mozart's sister (Nannerl) held her wedding reception here in the Gaststube, or dining room. With emphasis on homegrown décor, the hotel's fresh rustic interior was built using only timbers and materials from the Salzkammergut. What's more, each bedroom has its own cultured feel with contemporary design elements, and most have a balcony capitalizing on the dreamy views of the lake and Alps. Wine connoisseurs will treasure a trip down the narrow stone steps into the 16th-century vaulted cellar, where Austrian reds and whites are selected to be savored after a busy day of sightseeing and adventure.

Note: Hotel has elevator, bike rental, and recommended restaurant! Due to recent renovations, select the new Wolfgangsee deluxe room from mid-June. Add 1.65€ per person per night to price for bed tax. **PRICE**, Wolfgangsee Dbl deluxe from 178€. CC: VC, MC. GPS: N47 46.021 E13 21.851. Gasthof zur Post is situated on Mozartplatz in the heart of St. Gilgen, less than a 5-min walk to/fro the ferry dock and the Salzburg bus stop. **Drivers**, free parking (behind hotel); unload out front then have reception point you the way.

$$ **Hotel-Garni Schernthaner,** (Schwarzenbrunnerstr. 4, tel. 06227/2402, www.hotel-schernthaner.at, **free Wi-Fi** and use of Internet computer in lobby). These traditional Austrian digs, thoughtfully run by the Eisl family, have an indigenous alpine feel in the center of St. Gilgen. Upon checking in at reception (one floor up), you'll be greeted with a warm, genuine welcome by Anneliese, your host. In the evening, community service temporarily beckons her away from the hotel to close the parish church Saint Giles (Mozart's mother was baptized here in 1720). In the morning, Anneliese neatly places name cards at each table directing guests to their seats from which they can indulge in the breakfast buffet. But you'd better be quick, Hotel Schernthaner only has 17 rooms, all with balcony (higher floor equals better view), and guests are afforded free bicycle use to peddle around majestic Wolfgangsee and beyond. **Note:** Some rooms have a shower, some a bathtub, others have a combination of both. Hotel has elevator and sauna/wellness facilities (for a fee). Add 1.65€ per person per night to price for bed tax, and if staying only 1 or 2 nights add 3€ per person per night. **PRICE**, Sgl 54-58€, Dbl 96-104€, Trpl 138-146€, extra bed 12-15yr 25€, 2-11yr 19€. CC: VC, MC. Hotel Schernthaner is centrally located in St. Gilgen, less than a 5-min walk to/fro the ferry dock and the Salzburg bus stop. **Drivers**, unload out front then jump upstairs and notify Anneliese whether you'd like to park free outside or pay 3.70€ for a private garage.

$ **Hostel St. Gilgen,** [HI] (Mondseer Strasse 7, www.oejhv.or.at, tel. 06227/2365, GPS: N47 46.096 E13 22.039). Located meters from the shoreline and a two-minute walk from the ferry dock (follow lakeside path behind Mozart museum), this 40-room hostel is one of Austria's most popular in the HI family—a great way to experience the aquatic activities and splendor of Wolfgangsee for a cut-rate price. **PRICE** (includes sheets and breakfast but not the town bed tax of 1.65€ per person per night), dorm bed 24€, Sgl 37€, Dbl 60€. CC: VC, MC. **Note:** All rooms have shower-toilet. Cheaper when staying three or more nights. Must be a member or an extra charge (3.50€/night) will apply. Reception is typically open daily 17:00-19:00 and mornings Mon-Fri 8:00-13:00. Property is closed December 20-26, 2015. Oh, almost forgot, you can't beat their 6.50€ dinners (usually served at 18:00) but book it when making your bed reservation.

Mondsee, for town introduction, see page 98.

The warmest lake in the Salzkammergut, Mondsee (meaning Moon Lake) can reach a cozy 26-degrees Celsius (79°F) in summer, which probably has a lot to do with why it has become home base for the largest windsurfing and sailing school in the German-speaking world. **Note:** Surf free in select spots around town, log-on to FreeWifiMondsee.

Tourist information (Dr. Franz Müller Strasse 3, www.mondsee.at, tel. 06232/2270, May Mon-Fri 8:00-18:00—June & Sept Mon-Fri 8:00-18:00, Sat 9:00-18:00—July-Aug daily 8:00-19:00, Sat-Sun from 9:00—and Oct-April Mon-Fri 8:00-17:00) is located on the town side of the tree-lined road leading to/fro the lake.

Railers, to get to Mondsee from Salzburg, catch bus 140 from the Hauptbahnhof or Mirabellplatz (hrly Mon-Fri, every other hour Sat-Sun, 50-min trip, adult one way 6.50€, day ticket 13€, youth 15-18yr 4.50€/9.10€ and 6-14yr 3.30€/6.60€, www.svv-info.at), or from St. Gilgen catch bus 156 (20-min trip, adult one way 3.30€, day ticket 6.60€, youth 15-18yr 2.30€/4.50€ and 6-14yr 1.70€/3.40€, but plan ahead because bus departs irregularly, e.g. 3/day Mon-Fri, 1/day Sat, and zilch on Sun). **Drivers**, the A1 autobahn skirts Mondsee 25 km east of Salzburg—*Ausfahrt* Mondsee (exit 264).

St. Michael's Church (www.pfarre-mondsee.com), a distant relative to the neighboring 8th-century monastery, is glorious to visit. SOM fans will recognize its movie-set interior, and on hot days everyone will worship its air-conditioned feel. St. Michael's can easily be found in the center of town; aim for the twin spires: open Mon-Sat 8:00-19:00, and Sunday from 11:00 on account of Holy Mass.

Hallstätter See

Immensely scenic Lake Hallstätter is bendy like a seahorse and, if you didn't know any better, you'd swear you were in Norway. Similar to a Scandinavian fjord, the lake (8.6 km long, 2.2 km wide and 125 m deep) is surrounded by dramatic scenery, gigantic mountains having sheer cliffs that rise up from the cobalt-blue waters. The primary town on this alpine wet dream is **Hallstatt,** a confined but postcard-pretty village bang against a forested mountain, where time seems to have stood still for centuries. Indeed, this

community is mega-old! So old, in fact, an entire epoch has been named after it. The term "Hallstatt" refers to the transitional period from the Bronze Age to the Early Iron Age, constituting the lands of west-central Europe to the Balkans, circa 800-400 B.C. Thus Hallstatt, or the "place of salt," is one of the continent's oldest towns. Prehistoric peoples bore deep tunnels into the mountain and mined salt here; boats sent by wealthy traders and monarchs retrieved the "white gold" for a fee. Salt was vital to survival throughout the ages as the mineral was used to preserve foods, i.e. meat—essentially functioning as pre-refrigeration. Due to this unique history and its diverse natural landscape, the artifact-rich village and surrounding area (Hallstatt/Dachstein) has since 1997 taken its place alongside such venerated sites as the Komodo National Park in Indonesia and Uluru National Park (Ayers Rock) in Australia as an esteemed member of UNESCO's World Heritage List.

Hallstatt, situated 85 km southeast of Salzburg and 45 km beyond St. Gilgen, is a remote and petite village (population 900) that doesn't take long to stroll through. Drivers will either park in lot P2 by the salt mines or in lot P1 if staying the night. Railers will be escorted into town by Stefanie, the boat. **But note** that Hallstatt is dead in the off-season (Nov-March) when many businesses are closed.

In town you'll discover colorfully quaint houses lining the shore; a sleek church spire resembling the tip of a spear defining the skyline; the world's oldest salt mine (since 1200 B.C.); wads of camera-toting tourists in summer; and a peaceful cemetery accommodating Michael's chapel, a.k.a. the Bone House. Yikes! Oh, and it's best to have some bread on hand to feed the ducks and swans, or you may offend tiny hearts. And it's okay to fill your water bottle from the market square's double-barreled fountain.

Note: This year the traditional Corpus Christi (Fronleichnam) festival lands on Thursday June 4, 2015, beginning with Mass at 9:00 in the Catholic church followed by a resplendent procession of villagers then the boat parade at about 10:30 (lasting 2.5 hours, but double-check times in advance with TI in case of changes). Arrive early if you'd like to reserve a place on one of the sightseeing boats joining the waterborne spectacle.

Tourist information (www.hallstatt.net, Seestrasse 99, tel. 06134/8208, Jan thru June & Sept thru Dec Mon-Fri 9:00-17:00, July-Aug Mon-Fri 9:00-18:00, Sat-Sun 9:00-16:00) is located in the wood-paneled Sparkasse building at the main vehicular entrance (after tunnel turn left) to Hallstatt. Stop by here first (especially Drivers and those arriving by bus), pick up a map, meet friendly Teresa and her colleague and consume their local wisdom, choose from colorful brochures, use the public toilets (.50¢).

Internet: The whole of market square, or Marktplatz, is a **free Wi-Fi** hotspot.

Post Office: Mail your letters and picture postcards at the post office (Mon-Fri 8:00-13:00) centrally located in town at Seestrasse 169, across from Museum Hallstatt.

A **grocery store** ("Nah & Frisch," Mon-Fri 8:00-12:00 & 15:00-18:00, summer open all day without pause, Sat 8:00-13:00) is located opposite the Busterminal, meters from the TI at the main vehicular entrance to Hallstatt. Another option is the **Spar** market (daily 7:00-20:00) in the 'Gemischtwaren Handlung am See' shop by the market square.

Laundry: Have a coffee and wash at the small *Waschsalon* (daily 7:00-21:00, 7€/wash, 7€/dry) in the 'Gemischtwaren Handlung am See' shop by the market square.

Railers: From **Salzburg**, you can reach Hallstatt either by train from the Hauptbahnhof (change in Attnang-Puchheim, total journey 2.5hr, www.oebb.at, small groups purchase the Einfach-Raus-Ticket page 64) or more scenic catch the regularly scheduled bus 150 from outside the Hauptbahnhof shepherding you through the lake district to Bad Ischl (rail station) where you pick up a train to Hallstatt station (total journey 2.5hr). If

you're coming from **Vienna**, catch the train from Westbahnhof and change in Attnang-Puchheim (hrly until last train around 15:00, total journey 4hr, www.oebb.at). Upon arriving at **Hallstatt station**, you'll quickly realize you're on the wrong side of the lake—thus a cute boat named Stefanie (pictured) will be there to escort you (for 2.50€) across the lake to Hallstatt. By the boat dock is an info board with town map. You'll see the tourist information office is located on the other side of

Hallstatt, a 10-min walk. To get there, bounce straight off the dock then left around the pointy church; pass the market square on your right and the TI is straight ahead (through narrow lane, passing Gasthof Simony on the left) at the end of Seestrasse. **Note** that Stefanie's *last* pick up from the train station to Hallstatt is 18:50. Stefanie's first departure from Hallstatt to the train station is 6:50 (but 8:10 on Sun), then regularly throughout the day until its last departure at 18:15 (check times at the dock or with TI in case of changes).

Drivers: Hallstatt is a fair drive from downtown Salzburg, about 85 km (or 90 min), but wonderfully scenic—follow signs to St. Gilgen then Bad Ischl, Bad Goisern, Hallstatt. If you're coming from **Salzburg** on the A1 autobahn (heading east direction Vienna), take the Mondsee exit (No. 264) and drive along the lake to St. Gilgen then Bad Ischl, Bad Goisern, Hallstatt. If you're coming from **Linz/Vienna** on the A1 autobahn (heading west direction Salzburg), take exit No. 224 (Regau) to Gmunden then Bad Ischl, Bad Goisern, Hallstatt. **The road** approaching Hallstatt will funnel into a one-kilometer-long tunnel cutting through the mountain above town. To drive in Hallstatt during the touristed season, April-Oct, is *verboten!* (In the off-season, Nov-March, you can drive in Hallstatt but not park. In this case, drive through the tunnel, turn left and steer straight into town.) Since cars in Hallstatt are restricted to residents, you must park in one of the numbered pay lots outside town—I suggest you use P2. To get there, continue straight through the tunnel then turn right following signs to lot P2 (first 15 min free, 15 min to 1hr 3€, 1-2hr 5€, 2-3hr 6.50€, 3-12hr 7.50€, cash or VC/MC okay), within a 10-min walk of central Hallstatt and a Frisbee toss from the world's oldest salt mines (see next page). **Note:** If you have a hotel reservation, the parking situation is different for you, see Good Sleeps—Drivers.

Churches: There are two churches in town, Catholic and Protestant. Throughout the centuries the townsfolk have repeatedly changed denominations according to the trend, or who was in power. Today, most of Austria is Catholic, and so is Hallstatt. The Protestant church is situated on the waterfront, adjacent to the market square, and is recognizable by its spear-like spire (pictured). The much older, 14th-century Catholic church is the significant structure perched above the village. Here you will discover excellent views and the...

LAKE DISTRICT

Bone house, locally Beinhaus, (typically May till end of October daily 10:00-18:00, adult 1.50€, youth .50¢, ask for English info sheet, allow 10 min for a visit). For a chilling experience visit the house of bones in the cemetery behind the Catholic church, 105 steps above the market square. Dating from the early 18th century, a ghoulish custom

permitted graves to be cleared every 10-15 years to conserve what little land Hallstatt had available. Skulls were exhumed, cleaned, then left to bleach in the sun for weeks before being stored in the adjacent chapel (Michaelskapelle, a.k.a. Beinhaus), where oodles of calcium-deficient bones and skulls are on display in neatly stacked rows. Of the 1,200 skulls exhibited, some with teeth missing and grinning jaw bones, more than half have been ornately painted (mostly during the years 1780-1900) with flowery designs, oak leaves (symbolizing glory), laurel wreath (victory), roses (love), black crosses, and the name of the deceased identified on the forehead. Look for the darkest skulls; these are the oldest. The last skull to enrich the cranium collection was as recent as 1995, when the final request of a woman was honored to be placed in the house of bones, at the top of the heap, beneath the cross (identified by the year of her death, 1983). Today,

Catholics are allowed (since the 1960s) to choose cremation as a funeral rite, which bodes well for land-restricted Hallstatt. Whether you're pious or not, the Catholic church and its neighboring cemetery are must-see sites, and the lake views from here are enchanting!

Museum Hallstatt, (May-Sept daily 10:00-18:00—April & Oct daily 10:00-16:00—and Nov-March Wed thru Sun 11:00-15:00, allow at least 75 min for a visit, adult 8€, student 7€, senior 60yr+ 7€, family 18€, www.museum-hallstatt.at), features 26 rooms taking visitors on "A journey through the ages, 7,000 years of Hallstatt's culture and history": from past epochs to today's village of archeological discoveries. The journey begins with a 5-minute 3D film (pick out your glasses then push button for English), followed by an exhibit of 'human excrement' from the 4th century B.C., and

(in room 8) big and little kids alike will have fun with the four-way mirror (pictured).

Salt Mines, locally Salzbergwerk, www.salzwelten.at, open April 25 thru Nov 1, 2015, closed remainder of year—daily, April 25 thru Sept 20 9:30-*16:30, Sept 21 thru Nov 1 9:30-*15:00—*denotes departure time of last tour but you must be on the funicular railway at least 30 min before that to make it in time. All told, traveling to/fro mines and 70-min tour, allow three hours for a visit. **Price** (includes round trip on funicular and 70-min German-English tour of salt mine), adult 26€, student/senior 23.50€, youth 4-15yr 13€ (ages 0-3yr not permitted in mines), family 2+1 54€ or 2+2 65€ or 1+1 34€, discount with valid Salzburg Card and the Salzkammergut Erlebnis Card. The **funicular** railway (called the Salzbergbahn) is located at the south end of town (within a 15-min walk of the market square, Drivers park in lot P2) and is synchronized to run with the opening and closing of the salt mines (tickets to the mines can be purchased here at the station; note time of last funicular down). **Funicular & hikers**; salt mine only (without funicular) adult 19€, student/senior 17€, family 2+1 40€ or 2+2 48.50€ or 1+1 25€; round trip on funicular (without salt mine) adult 13€, student/senior 11.50€, family 2+1 27.50€ or 2+2 33€ or 1+1 17.50€. **Note:** By the funicular docking station, step out to the point of the tri-angle-shaped **skywalk** jutting from the mountainside high above Hallstatt for the **most awesome view in town**. Best on a clear day. Not for those who have a fear of heights!

With salt deposits being exploited as early as the 2nd millennium B.C., the Hallstatt mines are recognized (via carbon dating) as the world's oldest that are, astonishingly, still worked commercially today (by some 39 miners who yield roughly 550,000 cubic meters of salt per annum). Situated high above Hallstatt, deep in the mountain, the salt mines can be reached via one *steep* funicular (cable railway) followed by a 15-min walk past a pre-historic burial ground (to which the fertile findings here of some 4,000 peoples and their advanced tools confirmed the transitional period from the Bronze Age to the Early Iron Age, known as the "Hallstatt" era). Tourists throw on oversized miners' uniforms, march into the cool mountain (temperatures range between 7-10°C/44-50°F), explore subter-ranean cavities dug by prehistoric peoples, meet the "man preserved in salt" (discovered 1734), slide down two long wooden banisters (stairs also an option), and ride a bench on wheels out of the mountain. (If it's late in the day, don't miss the last funicular down the mountain otherwise plan on a 40-min trek, albeit picturesque and healthful.)

Boat Rides: The Hallstätter See Schifffahrt (ferry) company has been touring the lake's glacial waters since 1862, as well as operating the milk-run between Hall-statt (Markt) and the train station (Bahnhof) since 1881. Today, they have a fleet of four boats and you're welcome aboard. Consider the 50-min scenic excursion from Hallstatt to Obertraun (bottom end of lake) and back, adult 9€, youth 4-13yr receive discount—other excursions available; see ferry kiosk for details or go to: www.hallstattschifffahrt.at. The shortest and easiest lake jaunt is with Stefanie, the boat ferrying travelers to/fro the train station on the opposite shore, 2.50€ each way. At the train station dock, note the boat return times then go for a hike. A popular destination is the suspension bridge (Hänge-brücke) traversing the deepest part of the lake, 125 m (410 ft). The bridge is a short walk from the train station; have the boat captain point you the way. **Note:** If you're interested in renting an electric or muscle-powered (paddle) boat, you have a few summer choices around town: ask TI or your hotel reception for details.

Best Views: Hike above town following signs "Welterbe-Rundweg" to capture stunning vistas from ancient paths, two bridges and a waterfall (reach the first bridge in 15 min then trek another six min to reach the green bridge at the waterfall), or effortlessly climb the mountain via the funicular railway and step onto the skywalk for the **most awesome view in town** (see Salt Mines). Close and convenient, negotiate the 105 steps rising from market square to the Catholic church and graveyard. The scene, deepened by rows of wooden crosses spiked above immaculately tended plots dressed in a breadth of multicolored flowers, is right out of a movie. Another best view, this one pretty as a postcard, takes us to the "photo point" in the Römisches part (north end) of town that all the pros go to get that dreamy spread of Hallstatt. To get there, with your back to the front entrance of the Protestant church (recognizable by its spear-like spire), jog right and con-tinue straight a few minutes on the main lane as it climbs away from the market square and village center to the photo point ahead. You'll know it when you reach the perfect shot (best results in the morning).

Nature lovers should inquire at the TI for the plethora of unbeatable hiking and cave-exploration opportunities in this World Heritage region of Hallstatt/Dachstein (www.dachstein-salzkammergut.com), especially the over-the-edge adrenaline rush af-forded by the "5fingers" viewing platform overlooking Hallstätter See and the lake dis-trict. For nature junkies, consider the "4 Gipfelticket" or an all-inclusive Dachstein ticket for one fair price.

WWII buffs, don't miss the small and informal Tauchmuseum ('diving museum,' usually Mon-Fri 8:00-18:00, pay 1€ in antique shop at Pension Hallberg across from Mu-seum Hallstatt), in which oodles of Nazi medals, ordnance and weaponry were recovered from the bottom of the surrounding lakes by the museum's owner and his brother and now fill glass showcases, together with *fake* gold bars (that helped perpetuate the Nazi gold myth in these parts), in an upstairs hallway.

Good Eats: You can typically get a traditional and tasty meal at the **Grüner An-ger** (3-course menu from 12.50€, see Good Sleeps below); **Gasthof Zauner** (ivy-covered house at top of market square, 17:30-22:00, specializing in fresh lake fish); **Bräugasthof** (on the water's edge, some 60 meters south of Museum Hallsatt, sit inside beneath a wood-beamed ceiling or outside on the terrace within bread-tossing distance of graceful swans, May-Oct, cash only); or for more money you'll find **Im Kainz** in the Heritage Hotel (see Good Sleeps below).

GOOD SLEEPS: Hallstatt is idyllic, romantic, excellent for recreationists who enjoy hiking, cave exploration, climbing, boating. In peak season (April-Oct), Hallstatt is re-splendent in the warmth of summer, multihued flowers, and tourists. In the off-season (Nov-March), Hallstatt is dead, dark and cold. Unless you're a recreationist or on a spe-cial getaway (like a honeymoon or peaceful retreat), one night in Hallstatt will suffice. For a multi-night stay, first consider Pension Sarstein, located at the north, i.e. quiet, end of town.

As just mentioned, Pension Sarstein is located at the north end of town (near the "photo point" listed above in Best Views), the Grüner Anger is located at the south end

LAKE DISTRICT

of town, and the Heritage Hotel is between the two (meters from the market square and boat dock). To walk from one end of Hallstatt to the other, i.e. Pension Sarstein to Grüner Anger, is only 15 min.

Railers, since Hallstatt's train station is across the lake, you'll be arriving into town on Stefanie, the boat (2.50€/person each way).

Drivers, automobiles and Hallstatt are a bad mix. Thus, in 2011, it was approved that only residents be allowed to drive in town during the touristed months (April-Oct). In the off-season (Nov-March), however, Hallstatt is dead and (typically) open to every make and model—but you'll still need to park outside town, as explained below. Because of the driving difficulties hampering Hallstatt, I've listed the skinny on parking to get you to your digs with the least amount of fuss. And it starts with the Grüner Anger (see next page), where parking is free and easy for guests. Otherwise, continue straight out the one-kilometer-long tunnel cutting through the mountain above town and follow signs straight to the parking garage P1, designated for overnight guests. At lot P1, press the button "Hotelticket," take the ticket, enter and park in any available space. Mosey over to the Hotel Info point, near the parking entrance, and notify the attendant of your hotel reservations. If unattended, press the button to call up the hotel shuttle. A bus or mini van will arrive shortly to take you to your digs. The price to park is 9€/24hr 1-3 days (6€/24hr 4-7 days, 4€/24hr 8+ days), payable at the on-site automat, cash or CC. **Note:** After you've fed the automat for your stay, you're allowed to drive in/out of the lot as often as you'd like. The shuttle service is included in the parking fee, thus it is not required that you tip the driver (but if you feel the need to do so then by golly go for it). Before checking out of your digs, arrange with reception to be shuttled back to your car.

$$$$ Heritage Hotel, (Landungsplatz 101, www.hotel-hallstatt.com, tel. 06134/20036, **free Wi-Fi** and cable connection in room). These contemporary 4-star digs with flat-screen TVs and Nespresso coffee makers are ideally located on the boundary of market square and bang in front of the boat dock, greeting new arrivals into town, hence the hotel's address: Landungsplatz, or landing stage. A member of the "Castle Hotels and Mansions" association, the Heritage Hotel is actually a trio of heritage properties in Hallstatt: the **Kainz Haus** (main lakeside property with reception, sauna, breakfast, and in-house restaurant "Im Kainz"); the **Seethaler Haus** (with 11 double rooms, 3 suites, and sensational lake views due to the property's elevated position, is a short walk from Kainz); and the **Stocker Haus** (more than 5 centuries in age, is the oldest secular building in Hallstatt's historic center, with 6 rooms, a short walk from Kainz). Of the 34 rooms in the Kainz Haus, about 30 of these have lake views, and more than half have a balcony. Oddly, the few suites in the main building do *not* have a lake view. Five double rooms, conversely, have a small garden with terrific views to boot. When making your booking, reserve a room with a lake view. There is no extra charge for this room-type, but if you check in late (i.e. last), your request may not be fulfilled, thus arrive earlier rather than later to beat the bunch to your beautiful bed. **Note**: Check-in from 14:00, check-out by 11:00. Match your arrival date with the listed season to determine room rate (note that rates may vary slightly). High season (A): May-Sept and Dec 26 thru Jan 6 — Mid-season (B): April & Oct — Low season (C): Jan 7 thru March and Nov 23 thru Dec 23. On the hotel's Web site, click "Offers" to possibly find the right package for you. **PRICE** (does *not* include breakfast), **Sgl deluxe** 139€(A)/119€(B)/99€(C), **Dbl deluxe** 195€(A)/185€(B)/165€(C), **Jr. suite** (35-55 m², can accommodate up to 3 people) 325€(A)/295€(B)/265€(C), **Suite deluxe** (around 80 m², can accommodate up to 4 people in two rooms) 395€(A)/325€(B)/295€(C), breakfast buffet 15€/person. All major CCs accepted. **Railers**, your digs are meters in front of you after stepping off Stefanie in Hallstatt; (if you don't see the hotel, have the boat captain point it out to you). **Drivers**, follow directions under Good Sleeps—Drivers: park in P1, catch the shuttle to your digs.

$$ Grüner Anger, (Lahn 10, tel. 06134/8397, anger.hallstatt.net, **free Wi-Fi** in

room). This warmly run Austrian-style inn by Andrea and Gottfried Sulzbacher is a pleasant overnight choice for Drivers, who can park for free out front, and for anyone else seeking local hospitality in the 'green pastures' of Hallstatt, hence Grüner Anger (pronounce A like in Austria), at the south end of town but *without* lake views. Virtually a hop, skip and a jump from the tourist information office and the funicular railway lifting visitors up the mountainside to the world's oldest salt mines (page 78), Grüner Anger also affords its guests the use of free bicycles and a **recommended restaurant** with delicious 3-course menu options from 12.50€ (arrive before 19:30, consider the fresh lake fish grilled to palate-pleasing perfection by chef Andrea). **PRICE** (includes breakfast buffet; add 2€ per person if staying only one night), Sgl 59€, Dbl/twin 86-96€, extra bed adult 25€. CC: VC, MC. **Note:** Children up to 5yr are free with parents. **Drivers**, continue straight through the tunnel above town and (out the other side) drive a short distance farther then turn right to Grüner Anger. **Railers**, these digs are a 10-min walk from the boat dock in town, thus you can walk (have a local point you toward the salt mines) or call Grüner Anger ahead with your exact arrival time and Andrea or Gottfried will pick you up (if coming from the train station, and crossing the lake on Stefanie, show the boat captain your reservation and he will call Grüner Anger for you).

$$ Pension Sarstein, (Gosaumühlstrasse 83, www.pension-sarstein.at.tf, tel. 06134/8217, **free Wi-Fi** in common area). Caringly run by English-speaking Isabel and Lederhosen-wearing Klaus, this traditional bed-and-breakfast at the north end of town abuts the scenic shoreline of Lake Hallstätter affording its guests romantic lake views and a waterfront garden ideal for relaxing in lazy chairs and a gentle swim in the midst of waddling ducks and graceful swans. Rustic rooms with pine-wood furnishings accentuate this peaceful pension that guests awake from deep, revitalizing sleep to the quiet stillness of the morning *and* (often) stiff bath towels from being hung too long on the clothesline. **PRICE** (cash only, includes breakfast, add 5€ per person if staying only one night), Dbl 64-80€, Trpl 96-120€, family (4 pers.) possible. **Note:** These digs are typically always full; reserve your room well in advance. Request room with lake view and balcony. Since there is no formal reception desk here, it's best to give a general time of arrival when booking. If the outside door is locked upon your arrival, ring the buzzer to be let in. Because this is a multi-level property, there are a number of stairs to negotiate, i.e. there is no elevator! Borrow one their bicycles (free for guests) and increase your sightseeing possibilities, e.g. ride to Obertraun for a day trip (buy picnic goodies at Nah & Frisch or Spar grocery store on way out of town). Lastly, laundry service is available (i.e. Isabel/Klaus will wash your clothes) for a nominal fee. **Railers**, these digs are within a 5-min slightly uphill walk from the boat dock. On Stefanie, you'll see Pension Sarstein ahead on the right as you motor towards Hallstatt. **Drivers**, discuss the parking situation with Isabel—depending on the time of year and availability, you may have the option of parking for free a few hundred meters from the property.

LAKE DISTRICT

The Sound of Music
do-it-yourself tour

"The Sound of Music" (SOM), based on a true story, is arguably the most popular musical film of all time. A guidebook to Salzburg simply would not be complete without a tribute to its creation. With more than five years of experience as a SOM tour guide living in Austria, I've written the following step-by-step instructions so you can do the tour yourself, easily and efficiently, leading straight to the locations made famous by this timeless classic. You will save a tidy sum in comparison to paying for a commercial tour at around 38€ per person, essentially recouping the price of this guidebook several times over (depending on the size of your group). Additionally, my tour visits more sights and you're not rushed in doing so. (The commercial tour, for example, does not visit the cemetery or festival halls or Mirabell Gardens and only drives past a number of other sites. Where the commercial tour does earn a portion of its worth is by getting you to the lake district [25 km] outside Salzburg to visit St. Michael's Church at Mondsee, where the wedding scene was filmed. But, if you have wheels, even this value is insignificant.)

So come along, and discover SOM with HTB (Harriman Travel Books). But first, before we start our tour, let's begin with the basics.

SOM 101

The Movie: In 1963, a Hollywood scouting team began searching locations in the Salzburg region. Back in California, director Robert Wise was role casting. Mia Farrow auditioned for the role of Maria, Kurt Russell and Richard Dreyfuss tried out for the younger roles. Wise considered Sean Connery, Richard Burton and even Doris Day for leading roles before ultimately casting a group of relative unknowns. By spring 1964, after three months of exhausting rehearsals, the 250-person cast and crew arrived in Austria with a shooting schedule of six weeks. Everything was on cue, a seemingly watertight program, except for the weather—six weeks turned into a slog of 11! Upon completion, everyone returned stateside to wrap up the interior scenes on a Twentieth Century-Fox sound stage in Los Angeles. By that time, Friedrich (Nicholas Hammond) had grown 6 inches in 6 months thus Lisl had to stand on a box to appear taller. Marta (Debbie Turner) lost her two front teeth but the props department came to the rescue with substitutes.

Finally, to the elation of all involved, "The Sound of Music" was released in March 1965 and theaters everywhere were sold out. Julie Andrews and Christopher Plummer played the starring roles in the Rodgers and Hammerstein production, which won five Academy Awards: Best Picture, Director (Robert Wise), Sound, Film Editing, and Scoring of Music Adaptation.

Main Characters: One of my favorite scenes in the movie is when Maria meets Georg for the first time.

Herr von Trapp: "Why do you stare at me that way?"
Maria: "Well, you don't look at all like a sea captain, Sir."
Herr von Trapp: "I'm afraid you don't look very much like a governess."

Maria Augusta Kutschera (played by Julie Andrews) was born on a train en route to Vienna, Austria before midnight January 26, 1905. Maria aspired to be a nun and consequently became a postulant at Salzburg's esteemed Nonnberg abbey. It was here that she became aware of Georg von Trapp, a titled widower, when in 1926 he requested a home tutor for his third child (second-oldest daughter, Maria) who had become bedridden with rheumatic fever. The Reverend Mother Abbess responded to Herr von Trapp's request by sending him Maria, whom she felt wasn't ready for a sequestered life of chaste and obedience. The following year, on November 26, 1927, Maria and Georg tied the knot. (Note that it was not until 1936 that the von Trapps sang publicly as a family.)

Georg Ritter von Trapp (played by Christopher Plummer) was born on April 4, 1880 in the coastal town of Zara (present-day Zadar), Dalmatia located some 250 rugged kilometers south of Zagreb, the capital of Croatia. Yes, you read it correctly, Croatia! If Georg had been born within the last 95 years, there'd be no Sound of Music and we wouldn't be having this chat. You see, in those days, most of the Balkan Peninsula was aligned with the Austro-Hungarian Empire. Therefore, Georg had the privilege, as did his father, to be a naval officer serving greater Austria (remember, present-day Austria is landlocked with no access to seaports). Georg met his first wife, Agathe Whitehead, in 1910. She bore him seven children. Tragically, Agathe contracted scarlet fever and died in 1922, leaving the children motherless. Interestingly, Agathe was the granddaughter of (Englishman) Robert Whitehead, inventor of the torpedo. Robert had a workshop in the port town of Fiume (present-day Rijeka, Croatia), where Georg was stationed as a submarine commander. Thus Georg met Agathe and got married in Fiume, where their first two children, Rupert and Agathe, were born.

Maria Meets the Children: In actual fact, the seven children born to Agathe and Georg von Trapp were: Rupert (1911-92), Agathe (1913-2010), Maria (1914-2014), Werner (1915-2007), Hedwig (1917-72), Johanna (1919-94) and Martina (1921-51). In the movie, Hollywood immortalized them as:

Liesl, 16: She doesn't need a governess.

Friedrich, 14: He's impossible.

Louisa, 13: She's not Brigitta.

Kurt, 11: He's incorrigible, yet seemingly normal.

Brigitta, 10: She thinks Maria's dress is the ugliest she's ever seen.

Marta, 7 on Tuesday and she'd like a pink parasol.

Gretl, 5: She's practically a lady.

And as portrayed in the first part of the movie, the widowed captain's villa was surely a glum place of order and obedience. Before Maria, Georg did indeed call his children with a whistle (because of their large residence and gardens), just as he did to give commands to his sailors on the high seas. According to Maria (Georg's third child), to call Rupert, Georg blew one low note followed by one high note. Agathe's call was one low followed by two high notes, Maria was one low and three highs, and so on. When Georg required all the children, he blew a series of highs and lows ending with a low trill, but they never had to march or stand at attention. But after Maria's arrival from the convent, she loosened things up, introducing laughter and song to the household.

The Anschluss, America, and Movie History: In the early morning hours of Saturday March 12, 1938, Hitler's armies marched into Austria and declared the Anschluss, or annexation of the republic to the new German empire. Many Austrians dreamed of the day when both nations, Germany and Austria, would unite to form the greater Reich. There were many others, however, who desired no such idealistic fusion of the two nations and were content with their peaceful lives, i.e. the Trapp family.

Georg von Trapp, a reserved man possessing immense pride and wisdom, envisioned the harsh realities that lay ahead with the Nazis' tight grip on his beloved Austria. The regime ordered Georg out of retirement to serve the then German War Navy, or Kriegsmarine. This was, to say the least, not Georg's cup of proverbial tea. But Hitler's call to duty was a masked blessing for the von Trapps, prompting Georg to speak to each member of his family about their future, he asked 'What would become of us if we were to remain in the country?' In essence, either stay and say "Heil Hitler" or pack up and *get out!* With only the possessions in their rucksacks, the Trapp family pretended to go on a hiking trip to Italy and slipped through the Nazi web by train. And just like that, in a matter of hours, they had left everything behind: their personal items, valuables, mansion of a house, becoming refugees without a country. (Note: Pictured is Bahnhof Aigen, the

station from which the family boarded the train to Italy. Logistically it was an easy affair; the station literally sits behind the von Trapp estate.)

The family remained in Italy for about five weeks before heading to England, where they sailed 11 days to New York in September 1938. Dashing from country to country like fugitives was no easy task for the von Trapps, who had since swelled to nine children and Maria was pregnant with another on the way. (In 1929, Maria gave birth to Rosmarie, then Eleonore in 1931, and Johannes—president of the Trapp Family Lodge—in 1939).

Although they didn't speak English and only had a few dollars between them, life in America promised a new beginning far from Nazi tyranny. Moreover, the von Trapps were now a family of singers who could possibly strike it rich. Alas, six months later their visitor's visa expired without option for renewal. "When the Lord closes a door, somewhere he opens a window." Then, a stroke of luck, instead of having to return to Hitler's Austria, they were invited to perform concerts in Scandinavia.

The family toured Denmark and Sweden and Norway and then it happened: September 1, 1939, Hitler smashed his armies across the Polish frontier, kick-starting World War II. All borders in Europe were sealed shut and foreigners, even those with concerts planned, were asked to go back to wherever they came from. For the von Trapps, this was a possible death sentence.

Again, good luck fell upon the Trapp family as if God had personally dropped a miracle in their lap. Mr. Wagner, their manager in America, sent word that he arranged a new U.S. visa in sync with performances for a multi-state tour. In addition to the message, he sent money for a return voyage on the passenger ship SS Bergensfjord. Georg and Maria readily packed up their 10 children and, once again, cruised across the Atlantic Ocean.

On October 7, 1939, the SS Bergensfjord docked safely in Brooklyn. However, New York is not a city without drama, and Germanic peoples landing on American soil immediately after the Nazi boot stepped into Poland was, understandably, a sensitive issue with the immigration authorities. As a result, they were detained at Ellis Island while their paperwork was checked, and re-checked. While the *von Trapps waited behind bars, they once again pondered their future. Meanwhile, stories circulated of immigrants being detained for weeks on end before being shipped back to Europe, or Asia. One family even had to take refuge on a ship for months while it cruised between ports because no country would accept them. (*To view official government records of the passenger list and certificate of arrival, go to: http://www.archives.gov/boston/exhibits/von-trapp.html)

During their fourth day of confinement, the von Trapps received a final decision from the authorities. A guard appeared at their cell and told them they were *free* to leave. The jail door swung open and outside awaited the great land of opportunity. The sprung jailbirds toured America and became reasonably well-known as the "Trapp Family Singers" (performing regularly in the US, as well as in 30 other countries, until 1956).

In 1942, the von Trapps scraped $1,000 together and purchased an old farmhouse

SOUND OF MUSIC

(they called Cor Unum, Latin for "One Heart") on 600 acres in Stowe, Vermont, where the countryside reminded them of Austria. In 1950, they incorporated Cor Unum into the Trapp Family Lodge (www.trappfamily.com), which now comprises some 2,500 acres and 200 rooms, suites and guest chalets. Sadly, Georg never saw this dream unfold. Herr von Trapp, an extraordinary man whose surname would become as synonymous with Salzburg as Mozart, passed away May in 1947—he is buried in the family cemetery at the lodge. (Note: Maria departed us on March 28, 1987 and is buried with him at the lodge.)

Two years after Georg's passing, Maria penned the family's enterprising journey, "The Story of the Trapp Family Singers." Not believing it would ever amount to anything, Maria sold all the rights for $9,000. From the book sprang a two-part German film production in the 1950s called "Die Trapp Familie." The Germans subsequently sold the rights to the Americans, who (Rodgers and Hammerstein) made it into a long-running, hugely successful Broadway show. Twentieth Century Fox film studios bought the rights for $1.25 million and the rest is history. Interestingly, the movie aired for the first time on Austrian television around the year 2003, and many Austrians outside of Salzburgland have never heard of the von Trapp family.

THE TOUR

To wander Salzburg and behold its age-old sites is amazing. There's hardly a better way to spend a day in Europe, especially if the weather is nice. To complement this superlative plan, I have composed two do-it-yourself SOM tours: Walking, and Driving. **The Walking Tour**, as the name suggests, is easily achieved on foot and embraces all the Old Town attractions seen in the movie. (Note that I'll point out the **toilets** en route starting immediately with those at University Platz.) **The Driving Tour**, for those of you with wheels, can venture outside of Salzburg and marvel the remainder of the sights as well as the must-see lake district (Salzkammergut page 69).

Whether you only do one or both DIY tours, at the end of the day, the result is the same in this fairy-tale land of Salzburg: Your sightseeing discoveries, the same as those made by the Hollywood film scouts in 1963, will be the treasured memories of a memorable time. And these are for you to keep, forever.

Suggestion: Before you do the following tour(s), why not see the movie so the sights and sounds are fresh in your head? If you're staying at one of my recommended, SOM-friendly accommodations—such as YoHo (page 52), JUFA (page 53), Gabi's Apartments (page 55), or Hotel Wolf Dietrich (page 56)—then you're good to go. If you're *not* staying at one of the aforesaid accommodations, no problem; you're welcome to join the hostelers at YoHo in watching their free SOM screening every evening at 19:00, or stop by the JUFA hostel-hotel for their daily SOM screening at 20:00 (ask reception to start movie). Lastly, if you have time, watch the movie again post-tour. No matter how many times you've already seen the film, you'll see it with fresh eyes after you learn and experience first-hand the gripping history and sensational sights that have helped make this movie an enduring classic. For even more SOM flavor, consider an evening at **The Sound of Salzburg Dinner Show** (page 43), the **Marionette Theater** (page 44), or see the new musical that has come home to the Salzburg **Landestheater** (Provincial Theater, see TI or staff at your accommodations for latest performance dates).

Drivers, depending on your plans and where you're coming from, it may be better for you to do the Driving Tour first to avoid extra parking hassles in Salzburg.

Railers, you're not completely left out in the cold when it comes to the Driving Tour; you can do most of it (everything except the lake district) on your own by bike. (To rent a bike, flip to page 9 or ask TI for latest rental locations.) Start early and don't

SOUND OF MUSIC

forget to pack a picnic. Although touring by bike can be tiring, it's more comprehensive, healthier, and much cheaper than the commercial tours on offer for about 38€ per person. That said, if riding a bike isn't your thing, arrange a bus tour via the TI or your accommodations. Or, if there are a few of you, consider renting a car (which you will need to plan in advance, but with a car you'll have the option of visiting other exciting destinations, e.g. Berchtesgaden, Werfen, etc.—see Excursions page 64).

(DIY SOM) WALKING TOUR, University Platz to Mirabell—90 min

Let's start our Walking Tour in the middle of the Old Town on a square called University Platz, which doubles as a green market and is situated behind the rich-yellow facade of Mozart's birthplace. To get there, go to Getreidegasse (pedestrian shopping street) and stand at No. 9 facing Mozart's birthplace (page 22). Adjacent (left) is a shop-lined passage—walk through this to…

❶ University Platz, GPS: N47 47.969 E13 02.614. This is a great place to start our tour for two reasons: **(1)** availability of picnic items (Mon-Fri early till around 18:00, Sat till 14:00)—vendors offer everything from fruits and vegetables to meats and cheeses to grilled sausages (Würste) and various kinds of pretzels (around 3€ ea.), e.g. chocolate, cinnamon-sugar, pizza. **(2)** Remember the scene when Maria juggled the tomatoes and Gretl dropped hers? Filmed right here. **Note:** The golden facade you see is the back of ❹ Mozart's birthplace. Also note, the plaque above the *restaurant Zipfer reads: "In this house lived W. A. Mozart's sister Nannerl (widowed baroness von Berchtold zu Sonnenburg) from Oct 28, 1801 until her death Oct 29, 1829." (*If you cannot find the restaurant, face the back of Mozart's birthplace and the Zipfer is over your right shoulder.)

☞   To reach the next site, take the lane (Wiener-Philharmoniker-Gasse) running adjacent to the restaurant Zipfer. (Note that you'll immediately pass pay **toilets,** "WC," .50¢, on the right. The men's room, *Herren*, is downstairs.) The lane will empty into Max-Reinhardt-Platz, the southern end of the elongated…

❷ Festival Halls, locally Festspielhäuser, GPS: N47 47.904 E13 02.569. This enormous 17th-century structure, formerly the archbishop's stables and riding school,

extends the entire length of the block and houses Salzburg's three principal theaters. It was upon the stage of the middle theater that the Hollywood von Trapps sang their farewell songs before escaping to the cemetery. True to life, the von Trapps did sing here and win the group contest at the Salzburg Festival, as portrayed in the movie, but in 1936, not 1938 (and without Georg as part of the ensemble). Maria and the children may have had angelic voices but they never meant to sing publicly. With-

SOUND OF MUSIC

self-guided walk Sound of Music

Müllner Bräu

"Do-Re-Mi" steps

Mirabell Gardens

beer garden

Müllner-steg

Müllnerhauptstr.

Schwarzstr.

Mirabellplatz

Salzach River

Schrannengasse

Paris-Lodron-Str.

Wolf-Dietr.-Str.

Schallmooser Hauptstr.

St. Sebastian's graves of Mozart's father & wife

Linzergasse

9

H

Tour End

G

F

Mönchsberg

foot-bridge

Hanusch-platz

Getreidegasse

C

Old Market Square

K a p u z i n e r - b e r g

Hotel Stein

Steingasse

Imbergstr.

Tour Start

B

Uni-platz

A

1

Judeng.

Res.

7

Mozart-platz

i

8

Mozart Steg

Rudolfskai

Altstadt Garage

Neutorstr.

P

2

Toscanini Hof

3

4

E

D

Cathedral

Alpenstr.

Festival Halls

St. Peter's Church & Cemetery

cable railway

Fortress

Nonnberg Abbey

6

Berchtesgaden 25km

Sinnhubstr.

Untersberg

5

Erzabt-Klotz-Str.

Freisaal-weg

▲ Grocery store
✉ Post office
-- Walking tour

Harriman
TRAVEL BOOKS

1 University Platz
2 Festival Halls
3 Toscanini Hof
4 St. Peter's Cemetery
5 Untersberg Mtn.
6 Abbey, Nonnberg
7 Residenz Fountain

8 Mozart Steg
9 Mirabell Gardens

A Mozart's Birthplace
B Horse trough
C Mönchsberg Lift
D Kapitelplatz

E Cathedral Square
F Hotel Sacher
G Mozart's Wohnhaus
H Marionette Theater

SOUND OF MUSIC

out their blessing, the von Trapps were entered into the 1936 contest by an influential acquaintance at the last minute. Georg was not happy, and the family was frantic, as this passage in Maria's book, *The Story of the Trapp Family Singers* (p. 120-21 in my 1967 paperback edition), reveals: "My husband was aghast. He loved our music, he adored our singing; but to see his family on a stage—that was simply beyond the comprehension of an Imperial Austrian Navy officer and Baron." (Georg sternly protested the entry, but it was too late to withdraw. The moment had arrived.) "We stumbled onto the stage, stepping on our own and everybody else's feet ... In a daze we sang our three numbers, and none of us can remember today which ones they were. A gentleman down in the audience tried hard to look mildly interested but perfectly detached. Poor Georg! Our only wish, when we were off stage again, was to evaporate immediately, but we had to stick it out and wait for the awarding of prizes. As if in a fog, we saw the judges return from their conference. Silence settled over the vast crowd, and from afar we could hear the announcement: 'The first prize is awarded to the Trapp Family from Salzburg.' I remember that I didn't understand the meaning of these words, because I applauded wildly with the other people, looking blank. Upon instruction we had to go on stage once more and receive our prize, a diploma signed by the Governor of Salzburg. ...When my eyes searched around for my husband, his seat was empty. He had left in despair. Success or no success—the whole thing was a nightmare to him. It pained him bitterly to see his family on a stage, and only the solemn family resolution never, never to do such a thing again put his troubled mind at ease." Ironically, less than two years later, it was his family's singing ability that liberated them from Nazi subjugation. Georg, needless to say, learned to be a great fan of the "Trapp Family Singers." If time allows, I recommend you visit the halls via the one-hour, multilanguage tour. (For more on the Festival Halls, including tour times, see page 20.) **Optional:** At the other end of the halls you'll find the **B** horse trough (GPS: N47 47.964 E13 02.439), erected in 1695 as a princely bath for the arch-bishop's prized horses, briefly seen during the "Do-Re-Mi" curtain-wearing sequence (just before the tomato-juggling scene at University Platz). What's more, a few minutes farther along are the elevators accessing the **C** Mönchsberg (Monks' Ridge) observation terrace, where they also sang "Do-Re-Mi" (see Mönchsberg Lift page 31).

☞ Next stop, Toscanini Hof. Continue straight, in the direction you were walking, and bounce through the underpass.

❸ Toscanini Hof: In this secluded courtyard, named after one of Italy's great conductors, Arturo Toscanini (1867-1957), Herr Zeller, Hitler's Nazi boss of Salzburg, pulled up in his Mercedes looking for Georg (you'll fleetingly see the two giant-sized doors to your right). Herr Zeller hurriedly got out of his ride and goose-stepped into the right *corner to enter the staging area. Inside were Max and the children rehearsing for the upcoming folk festival. They informed the Nazi tyrant that Georg and Maria were still on their honeymoon. *Note: Beyond the atmospheric Felsenkeller bar.club (Wed-Thur 20:00-01:00, Fri-Sat 20:00-04:00) are doors that (when open) really do lead to the staging area. Also note that pictured on the wall left of the two giant-sized doors is the middle theater, or Felsenreitschule.

☞ From the Toscanini Hof, cruise through the passage (security pylon, left). Continue straight through the first courtyard (College of St. Benedict) and into the next one (St. Peter's monastery) toward the fortress. Stop at the forward arched passage (right corner).
To your right is St. Peter's Stiftskeller, Europe's oldest restaurant (page 46. If need-ed, in the Stiftskeller's open-air courtyard are *free* **toilets**—walk through the archway then go left to the end). When ready, skip through the passage and into...

❹ St. Peter's Cemetery, (daily 6:30-18:00, April-Sept till 19:00), the oldest active graveyard in Austria, is more than a 1,000 years of age. It is here the Trapp family hid during the escape scene. (Watch out for Rolf!)

Veer right and climb the graveled path to the Kata-komben, meaning "catacombs." Stand before them but don't go in.

From here, you can see that even if one of the gated vaults framing the cemetery were open, there'd be nowhere to hide. In reality, Hollywood hid the von Trapps in a studio but this cemetery inspired the director, Robert Wise.

Face the catacombs then shuffle left two wrought-iron vaults (LII) and you'll see (on the ground, middle right) the

name Canonicus Franciscus Wasner—this priestly man is the real Max Detweiler. He was not the conceited sponge the movie portrays. Father Wasner, whom the von Trapps first met on Easter 1935, was the family's spiritual advisor and musical conductor. It is absolutely essential when reviewing the history of the von Trapp family that Father Wasner be included, from winning the Salzburg Festival group contest in 1936 to their escape to Italy, to life in America and finally at Cor Unum (their homestead in Stowe, Vermont). Without Father Wasner, it is very possible the story would not exist. And here he rests before you, in Austria's most glorious graveyard. **Note:** For more on the cemetery, including a do-it-yourself tour of the catacombs, flip to pages 18 & 30.

☞   When finished visiting the cemetery, face Father Wasner then go left along the graveled path, paralleling the vaults, and straight out the gate. Climb the cobbled lane (Festungsgasse) past the cable railway (Festungsbahn) and Stieglkeller (which, by the way, has a recommended beer garden page 46). The view will develop into a wonder!

(**Readers participating** in my DIY tour of Salzburg, Mozartplatz to Mirabell, pick up from here:)

At the top the lane splits direction. Go left; this leads to the abbey (three min). Eventually you'll come to an archway; above it is St. Erentraud, first abbess, 712 A.D.—hence she's holding a representation of the abbey; (soon I'll show you her burial place in the crypt of the abbey church).

Go through the archway; follow the road as it bends right. Continue a bit farther and stop at the wooden benches beneath the huge maple tree. Spectacular view, no? Hopefully it's a clear day.

With your back to the wrought-iron gate (No. 4), gaze outwards to the forested hill in the valley with the canary-yellow structure nestling in the trees—this is the so-called Monats Schlössl (Month Villa), which belongs to Schloss Hellbrunn (where the "gazebo" is located) and can be seen on the Driving Tour. Now, move your eyes right and check out Untersberg mountain, resembling a colossal wave at Waimea Bay.

❺ **Untersberg:** Soaring (1,865m/6,117ft) above Salzburg's southern suburbs is perhaps Austria's most intriguing mountain: Untersberg. It is upon this landmass in the opening scene of the movie that Maria says she was singing. Maria explained passionately to the Reverend Mother Abbess that Untersberg is her mountain, and as a child she used to climb a tree and peer into the convent's garden (obviously with mega-powerful binoculars) to watch the sisters at work. Moreover, you'll see the uniquely shaped Untersberg numerous times in the movie with its lengthy plateau and V-shaped crevice. (Crevice not seen from this angle. In fact, only about half of Untersberg is in Austria and the V-shaped crevice marks the Bavarian frontier.) For example, when Maria is singing in the opening scene amongst the birch trees you'll see the V-shaped crevice in the background. (From that angle

she's actually in Bavaria, which contradicts her narrative to the Reverend Mother.) Also, you'll boldly see Untersberg when Georg and Maria are squabbling after the children fall in the lake. However, the most classic time is the final scene, when the von Trapps are escaping over the Alps into Switzerland—you can't help but notice Untersberg in the background vibrantly framed in Cinema Scope. Actually, Maria and the gang are climbing the mountainside adjacent to Hitler's Eagle's Nest. In essence, they are escaping into Nazi Southern Command. Bad move!

Let's get back to the opening scene. When Maria hears the bells chiming while on Untersberg, you now realize—from your view point, after the distance is calculated—that not only did Maria have bionic hearing, but she also must have been an Olympic athlete in training to even contemplate reaching the convent in time. No wonder she was late! (**Note:** For more on Untersberg, including riding the cable car to its summit, see page 35.)

☞ Turn around and enter through the wrought-iron gate (at No. 4) the nuns were twice seen behind talking to visitors.

❻ Abbey, Nonnberg: Dating from the 8th century A.D., the abbey on the Mountain of Nuns, or Nonnberg, is the oldest known convent in the German-speaking world. Together with St. Peter's monastery, this Benedictine abbey

represents the foundation of Christianity in Salzburg. Nonnberg abbey, true to life, is where Maria really assumed her postulancy; where she and Georg really got married (in the abbey church) on November 26, 1927 (he was 47, she was 22); and where Hollywood filmed three parts of the movie: **(1)** when Maria left the convent to meet the captain while singing "I Have Confidence"; **(2)** when the children were looking for Maria after she went missing; **(3)** and during the escape scene, when the Nazis demanded entry to search for the family of nine who seemingly vanished. (It's amazing how sneaky-fast the von Trapps were, going from the festival halls up to the abbey and back to the cemetery in just seconds.) **Note:** Because the convent is off-limits to the public, the movie crew was only given permission to film externally in and around the abbey church, which is where you are now. In front of you, the rose-marble portal leading into the church dates from 1497. Step inside and angle left through the pillars to see the Romanesque wall paintings (circa 1150 A.D.) that still survive from an earlier church that stood here before it was ultimately destroyed by fire. If it's dark beyond the glass, this means .50¢ is required for illumination. If the lights are on and the nuns are *singing in their secluded choir above, you've timed it just right. When ready, walk to the front right of the church and descend into the crypt (the burial place of St. Erentraud, Nonnberg's first abbess). ***Note:** For a heavenly highlight, time your abbey visit with the angelic voices of the nuns, who typically sing for 10 min Mon-Fri from 15:45, and for 30 min Mon-Fri from 17:15, Sat from 17:00, and Sun from 16:30.

(**Readers participating** in my DIY tour of Salzburg, head back the same way you came and "Mosey through the gate into St. Peter's Cemetery" page 18.)

☞ Let's resume our walking tour: Exit the church grounds and head back towards the cemetery the same way you came, passing the cable railway. Instead of returning through the cemetery gate, go right and follow the cobblestones down into ❶ Kapitelplatz—this is the asphalt plaza populated by souvenir stands and a huge chessboard. Continue straight through the arches into ❷ Domplatz, or Cathedral Square (**toilets** within arch-

SOUND OF MUSIC

way, left side); bypass the cathedral (to your right) and exit through the next set of arches. This vast graveled square is Residenzplatz, home of…

❼ Residenz Fountain, <u>GPS</u>: N47 47.918 E13 02.812. Smack-dab in the center of Residenzplatz is the fancifully fluid Residenz fountain—erected in 1658, it is said to be the most beautiful Baroque fountain north of the Alps. You'll recognize it from the scene

when Maria splashes water in the horse's face while singing "I Have Confidence" (she splashed the horse facing the "Hypo" bank, blue logo), and you'll see the fountain again immediately after the wedding scene when Nazi flags are hanging off the Residenz building (with its three stories of windows) and German soldiers marching through the square. Can you imagine the older locals who unknowingly went into town that morning to do some shopping? They almost certainly would have collapsed at the mere glimpse of the Wehrmacht troops and their high-kicking jackboots. *Déja-vu!* (**Note:** The fountain is covered for winter, typically from early Nov until the end of March.)

Time to throw on your specially tailored 'play clothes'

☞ Beyond the fountain, in the next square, you'll see a statue of Mozart—walk past him and angle downhill toward the river. Cross with the traffic light and step onto the footbridge. This is the…

❽ Mozart Steg, <u>GPS</u>: N47 47.963 E13 02.924. On this iron footbridge, built in 1903 and named after the legendary Amadeus, the opening scenes of the "Do-Re-Mi" curtain-wearing sequence were filmed. When you're about two-thirds of the way across, turn around for a stunning view. (The film crew capitalized on the view by positioning themselves off the bridge half way to the forward traffic light.) Once you've reached the end of the bridge, you'll remember the kids enthusiastically bopping from railing to railing and frolicking along the lush riverbank.

(**Readers participating** in my DIY tour of Salzburg, return to Mozartplatz and continue from there, page 14.)

☞ To reach the next and last site on our walking tour, cross at the forward traffic light and go left. Continue straight some distance to the next intersection, <u>GPS</u>: N47 48.083 E13 02.699. Once here, to your left will be the main bridge into the Old Town and to your right the Hotel Stein. (For an eye-popping view, visit the Stein Terrasse page 38.)

Keep trekking forward (on right side of street). Ahead on the left, the flowered balconies and flapping flags belong to the **❻** Hotel Sacher Salzburg (page 58), where Julie Andrews and director Robert Wise stayed during filming.

Continue straight. Weave your way past the people waiting at the bus stop (Theatergasse) and halt on the corner. The building over your right shoulder is **❼** Mozart's Wohnhaus (page 26), where his family moved to in 1773. The Hotel Bristol across the street (at your one o'clock) is where Christopher Plummer and the children stayed.

What you need to do now is rambo the triple-wide street in front of you to the other side, where the bus shelters are. Once it's completely clear of oncoming traffic and perfectly safe, *go!*

Great job. We're going to continue straight, but if you were to go left toward the traffic light then right around the corner, the first building you'd reach is the  Marionette Theater (page 44). It was these puppets that inspired the Lonely Goatherd sequence in the movie.

Continue straight ahead and pass between the two sets of Greek-inspired statues marking the entrance into the marvelous...

❾ Mirabell Gardens, (GPS: N47 48.294 E13 02.530), a jewel of landscape design, where diehard SOMers go bonkers and I tend to lose guests. Thus, I will end our walking tour here so you can enjoy the splendor at your own speed. But first, I'll explain a few things before bidding adieu.

Maria and the children skipped all through these gardens, as I'm sure you will, too. First, you probably recognized those Greek statues as the scene when Maria and the kids synchronized an arm-raising get-together. Go to the fountain in front of you where you saw them crisscrossing one another. Notice the string of linden trees to the left. On hot days they provide cool sanctuary. Head over to them and continue along the tree-lined path until the dirt changes to pavement. <u>Stop</u> here. In front of you (right) should be a wrought-iron fence enclosing the rose garden.

At this junction, all points are within striking distance. To your left is the ivy arcade the kids ran through. To your right, where the path arcs into the grass, you'll capture a postcard-perfect view (with the splendor of the gardens, skyline of the Old Town, and the majesty of the Alps at your photographic disposal). Straight ahead is the Pegasus (winged horse) fountain they ran around (climb the 15 steps to its left and cross the wooden bridge to find the dwarf they patted—first on left, having glasses, mouth open, holding hat), and beyond the fountain are the "Do-Re-Mi" steps (on which the adjacent picture was taken). The flanking unicorns are great to pose on. Have fun! **Note:** In winter, the gardens are half closed—you can see the sites but not fully experience them. For more info on the gardens, flip to page 25. For info on the Do-Re-Mi scene in the alpine meadow, see "SOM fans" on page 68.

(DIY SOM) DRIVING TOUR,
Anif to Moon Lake—2 hours

There are five sites in this section, four are in Salzburg and the fifth is in the lake district (Salzkammergut page 69). A suggested amount of time to visit is written for each site. The route is fairly simple to navigate and the countryside is delightful to behold, especially in the lake district. **Note:** Choice picnic spots include Schloss Hellbrunn (second stop) and anywhere in the lake district (last stop). Regarding the latter destination, if the weather's nice, bring your bathing suit.

Drivers, I've written simplified directions from site to site for you follow.

Railers, don't think you're excluded from the driving tour, you can, in fact, see four out of the five sites in this section (everything except Mondsee in the lake district) on your own by *bike. (To rent a bike, flip to page 9 or ask TI for other rental locations.) Your route, though, will be different to that of Drivers. Pick up one of the fold-out city maps from the TI and get yourself to Freisaalweg, a graveled recreational path southeast of the fortress. This will turn into Hellbrunner Allee, which runs past Schloss Frohnburg and concludes at Schloss Hellbrunn. From here, ride through Anif to reach the Water Castle before backtracking to Schloss Leopoldskron. (Try to fit in the Postscript at the end of this tour if possible.) Start early and pack a picnic. Although touring by bike can be tiring, it's more comprehensive, healthier, and much cheaper than the commercial tours on offer for about 38€ per person. (*Note: If riding a bike isn't your thing, arrange a bus tour via the TI or your accommodations. Or, if you're a small group, consider renting a car.) **To reach the fifth site** (Mondsee) in the lake district from Salzburg, catch bus 140 from the Hauptbahnhof or Mirabellplatz (hrly Mon-Fri, every other hour Sat-Sun, 50-min trip, adult one way 6.50€, day ticket 13€, youth 15-18yr 4.50€/9.10€ and 6-14yr 3.30€/6.60€, www.svv-info.at). **Suggestion:** During the week (i.e. *not* Sat/Sun because of limited buses), first ride bus 150 from Salzburg to St. Gilgen on Wolfgangsee (page 70, buy day ticket from driver), spend the day here (e.g. ride boat across lake to Sheep Mountain and back), then catch the last bus 156 from St. Gilgen (around 18:05) to Mondsee (20-min trip)—there's much less to see and do in Mondsee (page 75) thus a visit won't take long—but don't miss the last bus 140 departing Mondsee (around 20:30) back to Salzburg. (**Note:** Double check times and prices in advance with staff at your accommodations or TI in case of any changes.)

☞ Let's begin our driving tour at the Water Castle (GPS: N47 44.768 E13 04.049), located in the southern suburb of Anif. If you're coming from the city, have the TI or staff at your accommodations point the way. If you're coming from outer Salzburg, exit the A10 autobahn at Salzburg-Süd and follow signs to Salzburg/Anif. At the first set of lights turn right, direction Hallein. Coming up on the left, just past the margarine-colored

Hotel zum Schloßwirt (first big structure on left), is a short cobbled driveway before a gated entrance. Park momentarily in the driveway facing the…

🔟 **Anif Water Castle,** (1 min suggested). Built in the 17th century as a residence for the bishops of Chiemsee, this neo-Gothic water castle (sitting behind the massive tree) is briefly featured from the air in the opening shots of the movie. Besides its SOM fame, the castle can also been seen near the end of the 1974 movie thriller "The Odessa File" starring Jon Voight. Since the castle is privately owned, tours are *not* possible. From the gate, capture a photo. However, make it snappy, notice the golden plaques on either gatepost—they're informing you in three languages to 'beat it'!

☞   To reach Schloss Hellbrunn (<u>GPS</u>: N47 45.790 E13 03.847), go back to the traffic light and drive straight through the intersection into the spick-and-span village of Anif. On the other side of town is the Salzburg Zoo (right), and a few hundred meters farther is the Salzburg city-limits sign, make the next right at the end of the golden wall.

Soon you'll pass a small parking area within the walls to your right; continue straight past the second parking area (right) and at the third parking area (right) find a space and cut the engine. (Take a ticket: first 30 min are free, up to 2hr/2€, 3hr/2.80€, max 3.60€.) Walk through the palace's pointy back gate (nice photo opportunity to the front facade) then go left and the gazebo will be to your immediate right. From here, consider a stroll through the gardens. Unpack your picnic? **Note:** Salzburg Card holders receive free admission into the Schloss, trick fountains and zoo pages 32-33.

⓫ Schloss Hellbrunn, (10 min to half a day suggested). Some 20 years ago the gazebo was moved here from the private gardens of Schloss Leopoldskron. Now accessible to the public, more than 300,000 fans visit the gazebo annually to relive the harmonious scene "Sixteen Going on Seventeen" performed by Rolf (Dan Truhitte) and Liesl (Charmian Carr, who at the time was 21 going on 22). You may have noticed the gazebo looks

smaller; that's because this one was only used for external shots and a second, bigger prop was used on the set in Los Angeles. If you're jiggling the door handle to get in to dance on the benches, you'll be disappointed to know that it's always kept locked since previous, equally enthusiastic visitors have been carted off with sprained ankles and broken limbs. Case in point, Charmian Carr slipped and fell while rehearsing the scene and her foot went through a glass window pane. Crew members wrapped a bandage around her ankle and said keep going, "The show must go on." **Note:** No part of the movie was filmed at this location. When facing the gazebo, *free* **toilets** are behind you, the zoo is left at the end of the tree-lined path, and the green shield to your right explains a little more. For the history of Schloss Hellbrunn, flip to page 32.

☞ Return to the main road, go right and continue in the direction of Salzburg. After 1 km start looking to your right for Schloss Frohnburg—this is the estate enclosed within

golden walls, across the meadow, behind a row of trees. (Don't confuse it with the golden estate with white trim straight ahead.) Alas, there's nowhere to pull over, so drive slow and have your camera handy. What's more, a brief but magnificent view to the fortress will open up in front of you. (**Cyclists**, you'll get a much closer look at Frohnburg because the graveled bike path, Hellbrunner Allee, passes directly in front of the estate.)

⓬ Schloss Frohnburg: You'll recognize this estate in the movie as the front of the von Trapp villa. Remember when Maria approached the villa while singing "I Have Confidence" and swinging around those obviously *empty* bags before peering through the gate? You may also remember when the family silently pushed their vehicle out the gate, only to find Herr Zeller and his Nazi boyfriends there to greet them. (The Gestapo were tipped off by the family's butler.) And when Georg ripped down a long Nazi flag

SOUND OF MUSIC

hanging from the front facade after returning home from his honeymoon. Although it's difficult to recognize, these were not the only scenes filmed here. Schloss Frohnburg was also used (in conjunction with Schloss Leopoldskron, our next stop) as the back of the house (backside of Frohnburg cannot be seen from the road). In fact, if you don't see the lake, the scene was filmed at Schloss Frohnburg. For example, when Rolf throws pebbles at Liesl's window,

and when Georg (who is facing the lake) tells the kids to get their dinner, they hustle past him and into the back of Frohnburg. **Note:** Most all interior scenes of the von Trapp villa (and abbey) were shot on a Twentieth Century-Fox film set in Century City, Los Angeles. Historically, Schloss Frohnburg dates from the 17th century and was used as a country manor by the archbishops. Today, the estate accommodates students and study rooms from the Mozarteum (www.moz.ac.at), or Salzburg University of Music, Theater and Visual Arts. The university consists of several properties around Salzburg and has an international student body of 1,600. Maybe it's something for you or someone you know?

☞   At the upcoming intersection turn right, then make the first left onto Fürstenallee. At the junction ahead, go left (this is still Fürstenallee). Continue to the second set of lights and turn left (Sinnhubstrasse). On the right you'll have an impressive view of the fortress. Lower your eyes and you'll see a lone cottage in the meadow. This formerly belonged to the town executioner. Perhaps nobody wanted to hang out with him. (Pause for laugh.) The last person to wear the noose in Salzburg was in the early 1800s on the knoll behind the cottage. (If you've done my DIY Salzburg tour, Mozartplatz to Mirabell [page 11] you'll know that Joseph Mohr [of "Silent Night" fame] was born on Steingasse in the New Town. Interestingly, Salzburg's last hangman was Joseph Mohr's godfather.)

Continue straight; the road will narrow into an Einbahnstrasse, or one-way street. At the second traffic light turn left onto an even narrower road (Leopoldskronstrasse). At the forthcoming junction go left, following the sign Schloss Leopoldskron. Pass the Freibad Leopoldskron (community pool) and make the subsequent right into Firmianstrasse. Since this is a one-way road, watch out for cars heading your way and immediately pull into the corner *lot and park (but before you get out of the car, grab some bread for the ducks and swans). *Note: The lot is generally reserved for customers of Marchhart's Thai-Fish-Steak restaurant but it's closed Sun-Mon and doesn't open until 17:00 Tue-Sat.

Mosey some 200 meters on Firmianstrasse to the concrete vehicle barriers and join the lakeside path. Walk said path another 180 meters along the lake until you reach the oak tree growing out of the water, GPS: N47 47.180 E13 02.205.

From either side of the tree you're rewarded with a memorable picture of the fortress framed behind the palace (like the pictured inset). If you happen to be at the lake when a tour group arrives, notice how the guide stops the group well short of this best-picture spot. Time is money, ya know.

⓭ Schloss Leopoldskron, (20 min suggested, mostly because of walk). Originally built in 1736 for Prince-Archbishop Leopold Firmian, this stunning Rococo structure represented the back of the von Trapp villa (facade facing lake). No doubt you'll remember what scenes were filmed here. My favorite is just after the kids fell in the lake, when Georg interrogates Maria over children in trees and tailored curtains. After bitter squabbling, Maria exclaimed: "I am not finished yet, Captain!" Flustered, Georg replied: "Oh, yes you are, Captain!"

For the actors and crew, though, filming the boat scene wasn't as smooth as it appeared on screen. You see, little 5-year-old Gretl couldn't swim, so it was planned for Maria to sit with the little one and when they fell overboard Maria would immediately carry her to shore. Simple, right? Well, when they all stood up, Maria lost her balance and fell backwards off the boat. Gretl, on cue, fell forward and instantly sank (head to the bottom, one of her legs straight up in the air)! The scene cuts to an open-mouthed Georg then back to the kids, but only six are visible (and Maria is behind the boat not in the picture). The scene once again cuts to Georg, at which time a crew member jumped in to save Gretl from drowning (obviously edited from the film). When the scene cuts back to the kids, Louisa is cheerfully carrying Gretl to safety. Tragedy averted!

And after all these years, Gretl (Kym Karath) says she's "still not fond of the water after that experience." And who would, it took *four* takes to get the scene: fall in the lake, dry off, do it again. And that water was "freezing" cold, according to Liesl (Charmian Carr), who recalled her frigid feelings some four decades later as if they were yesterday.

Although this location was used exclusively for its lake scenes—the exterior of Leopoldskron palace is never seen in the film (the exterior that you do see is actually Schloss Frohnburg)— Boris Leven (production designer) was inspired by the palace's sumptuous mirrored Venetian room thus he recreated it in Los Angeles for the grand ballroom scene.

Today, Schloss Leopoldskron houses the Salzburg Global Seminar, an international conference center (www.salzburgglobal.org), as well as the highly rated Hotel Schloss Leopoldskron (www.schloss-leopoldskron.com).

In winter, the lake freezes over and throngs of locals keenly use it as a giant ice rink. In summer, the lake is a popular place to go for a stroll, jog, or kick back and cast a line (widely caught fish are carp and pike).

☞ To our next and last venue, roughly a 45-min drive, will deliver us from Salzburg to Mondsee (Moon Lake) in the wonderfully scenic Salzkammergut, or lake district. Thus I recommend you supplement this section with the Salzkammergut chapter, page 69.

1) From the parking lot, pull briefly onto Firmianstrasse, turn right so you're once again on Leopoldskronstrasse, then make a quick left onto Leopoldskroner Allee (as you make the turn the gated entrance into Schloss Leopoldskron will be to your right).

2) At the fork ahead go right, passing the executioner's cottage again. (Notice the palatial digs on your right—this is the Altenheim, or old folks' home.)

3) Turn left at the traffic light and follow the road (right) around the bend then yield left at the junction (onto Erzabt-Klotz-Strasse).

4) At the next set of lights turn left (Petersbrunnstrasse), where the abbey's red onion-domed steeple will present itself divinely. Go straight through the forward lights and cross the river.

5) At the next traffic light turn right following the sign to St. Gilgen. At the second traffic circle ahead turn left. Follow this road 1.5 km (about 1 mile) and you'll come to the major intersection of Linzer Bundesstrasse; turn right here (before it is a Hofer grocery store and the street Eichstrasse).

6) You'll only be on Linzer Bundesstrasse for half a kilometer—get in the right lane—after crossing the railroad tracks follow the sign right to St. Gilgen. This road (Minnesheimstrasse) will snake its way above Salzburg and eventually straighten out, escorting you through some of Austria's most striking countryside.

7) After 15 km (just after the town of Hof) you'll reach the inviting waters of Fuschlsee (page 69), the beginning of the Salzkammergut.

8) Keep driving towards St. Gilgen, located another 12 km on the shore of the next lake, Wolfgangsee (page 70). The moment you see the lake, pull over at the rest area. From here you can capture a similar image as the one briefly featured from the air in the opening shots of the movie. Another SOM sight is the pointy mountain with a structure planted at its summit. Maria and the children were seen steaming up the side of this mountain during the "Do-Re-Mi" curtain-wearing sequence on the Sheep Mountain Railway (page 73).

SOUND OF MUSIC

9) Exit the rest area and descend towards St. Gilgen. At the bottom, go around the turning circle direction Mondsee. You're now on Austria's "Romantic Road."

10) Along the route you'll pass the privately owned Schloss Hüttenstein, an enchanting mustard-yellow castle perched upon a forested knoll. Behind the Schloss is Krottensee, an idyllic lake named Turtle. Below the castle is Schlossmayrhof, a lovely farmhouse bed-and-breakfast run by the Zopf family (rooms have shower-toilet, balcony; cash only, Dbl from 63€, apartment available, tel. 06227/2380, www.schlossmayrhof.at).

11) Soon you'll reach the blue waters of Moon Lake, locally Mondsee. As you get closer to the town of Mondsee, situated on the distant shore, you'll spot what you came for: the twin steeples of St. Michael's Church.

12) Upon arriving in Mondsee, veer right following the sign to Mondsee-Süd. Your best place to park is across from the gas station (ahead, turn left, <u>GPS</u>: N47 51.177 E13 20.919). If the lot is full, park adjacent to the lake. (If you do park at the lake, ignore step 13 and walk the tree-lined road straight into town, to the church.)

13) After parking, walk the lane right of the gas station, following the green sign pointing Zentrum. Take this into town; you're aiming for the twin-steepled church. The asphalt lane will connect with a graveled path skirting an extensive field. Take this path to the tree-lined road on the opposite side and go left into town.

⑭ Mondsee: (The strudel stop, 30 min to a few hours suggested. If the weather is nice, consider a swim; Mondsee is the warmest lake in the Salzkammergut, reaching

26-degrees Celsius, or 79°F, in summer.) Translating to Moon Lake, Mondsee has to be romantic! The main town of concern here, and the reason for busloads of tourists, is the lake's namesake: Mondsee. Even though the Romans settled the town nearly 2,000 years ago and monks officially established it in 748 A.D., Mondsee didn't make any real headlines until 1965, when the movie "The Sound of Music" premiered. It was in the town's Baroque church (St. Michael's) that Hollywood married Georg and Maria von Trapp. When film scouts arrived in Salzburg in 1963, one of their target locations was a church for the wedding scene. However, most churches weren't hip to the idea; only a few would allow filming. Of their limited choices, film scouts chose this one. The following year the cast and crew arrived to shoot the scene. St. Michael's Church was wonderfully ornamented; extras filled the pews while an organ played and the nuns sang "How do you solve a problem like Maria...." We all remember the scene when Maria elegantly paced the nave in her long, flowing white gown to meet her beloved sea captain waiting patiently by the altar. **Note:** St. Michael's is open Mon-Sat 8:00-19:00, and Sunday from 11:00 on account of Holy Mass. Public **toilets** are located at the side of the Rathaus, or town hall, which is directly opposite Café Braun (mauve-colored facade; if you're going to Café Braun for a strudel, use their facilities). Across from St. Michael's you can find **scrumptious strudel** served with vanilla ice cream at Café Braun, locally known as the best. (According to the owner, Frau Braun, the SOM film crew used the second floor of her building as a rehearsal/dressing room.) After strudel, stroll along the tree-lined road to the lakeside promenade. It's time well spent.

That's a wrap, folks!
I hope you enjoyed the tour.
So long, farewell, auf Wiederseh'n, good*bye...*

To get back to Salzburg (25 km), the A1 autobahn is conveniently located on the north side of Mondsee. But **note** that vehicles traveling on the Austrian autobahn system are required to have a "Vignette," or toll sticker (page 102).

Postscript,

❶ **Trapp Villa:** You've seen all the SOM movie locations made famous by Hollywood, but what about the *real* von Trapp villa? Dating from 1863, this historic property was not used in the filming of the movie (for reasons explained below) but today it is open to travelers seeking a unique overnight experience.

Idyllically set within an *eight acre forested reserve in the Salzburg suburb of Aigen, the 14-room von Trapp villa is significant because it is here the story truly began in 1926 when a determined 21-year-old Catholic girl from the convent arrived to care for the captain's sick daughter. (*City's largest privately owned park.)

Georg and the children had moved here in 1923, where the family remained until Hitler's fascist army marched into Salzburg 15 years later. After the von Trapps fled Austria, the Nazis seized the villa. Heinrich Himmler, head of all Nazi police forces, was especially fond of the property and resided here when in town on "business." At this time the villa's leafy quaintness was sacrificed to a cordon of armed guards and barbed wire. Postwar, a religious order, the Missionaries of the Precious Blood, purchased the villa and kept it secluded from the community. Until now! The missionaries leased the property to a hospitality group that opened it to the public as **Villa Trapp** (bed-and-breakfast-style accommodations, tel. 0662/630-860, www.villa-trapp.com, reserve online with booking site for best rate).

Not only will you have the opportunity to sleep in the family's former bedrooms, but you'll also have the possibility to enjoy a specially prepared SOM dinner in the family dining room (where the children promptly gathered for meals on whistle command) and to get married in the house chapel (presently set in Georg and Maria's former bedroom—note that the location of the original chapel, where Father Wasner gave Easter Mass in 1935 when he first met the Trapp family and discovered their exceptional singing ability, is now the breakfast room). Although no actual furnishings from the von Trapp household remain, the villa is indeed in original condition—including the parquet flooring and the tall bending staircase whose wooden hand-railing repeatedly entertained the seven youngsters as a thrilling slide when their father wasn't looking—and outfitted with period furniture and fixtures as well as photos of the von Trapps and some family items.

Note: Because Villa Trapp is a private residence reserved for the exclusivity of its overnight guests, it is *not* open to sightseers seeking to tour the property.

GPS: N47 47.347 E13 04.906. **To get there**, Villa Trapp is located at Traunstrasse 34 in the suburb of Aigen, 3 km southeast of Salzburg's Old Town. **By taxi** from the Old Town is roughly 12€. **Railers** (if you're carrying a valid Salzburg Card then I suggest traveling by bus—see "By bus" below, otherwise) from Salzburg's central station, there's a regularly scheduled train (depart-

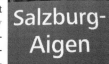
Salzburg-Aigen

SOUND OF MUSIC

ing every 30 min Mon-Sat, hourly on Sun) to Bahnhof Aigen (from which the von Trapps originally "escaped" the Nazis in 1938), 9-min trip then 9-min walk. From Aigen station bounce down the steps, through the underpass to the other side of the tracks, and up the steps. Veer right, go straight a few meters then right around the corner and follow the whitewashed wall all the way to the intersecting street and right around to the front gate of Villa Trapp nestling in the trees. **By bus** from the city, hop on #7 direction Salzburg Süd and get off at Bahnhof Aigen (train station from which the von Trapps originally "escaped" the Nazis in 1938), 10-min ride (bus departs Hanuschplatz and Mozartsteg every 10 min, and every 20 min after 19:00 Mon-Sat and all day Sun). From Bahnhof Aigen, it's less than a 10-min walk—jog across the street, down the steps, through the underpass to the other side of the train tracks, and up the steps. Veer right, go straight a few meters then right around the corner and follow the whitewashed wall all the way to the intersecting street and right around to the front gate of Villa Trapp nestling in the trees. **Drivers**, parking is free on the property. **If you're heading** west direction Salzburg on the A1 autobahn, exit at Salzburg Nord. Drive towards Salzburg. Continue on this busy avenue (Salzburger Strasse turning to Vogelweiderstrasse) all the way to the end. At the traffic light, turn left. Ahead, under 1 km, veer right onto a one-way section of road (Ignaz-Härtl-Str, after gas station) then go right at the forward junction. Drive this heavily trafficked road 1.5 km (about 1 mile) to the end and turn left (direction Schloss Hellbrunn, Zoo). This will put you onto Aigner Strasse, leading to Aigen. Continue straight and at the second traffic light (Blumaustrasse), turn left. Drive beneath the train tracks (on which the von Trapps originally "escaped" the Nazis from nearby Aigen station in 1938), follow the road right around and make the second right into Traunstrasse. At the other end of this residential street, beyond the whitewashed wall, is Villa Trapp (right) nestling in the trees. **If you're coming from** the A10 autobahn, exit at Salzburg-Süd and drive towards Salzburg. After about 4 km turn right (immediately past the Park+Ride) direction Aigen. Continue straight and cross the river. Go left on the upcoming traffic circle, putting you onto Aigner Strasse leading to Aigen. Continue straight—you'll soon drive beneath the train tracks on which the von Trapps originally "escaped" the Nazis from nearby Aigen station in 1938—about 3 km ahead at the 4th traffic-lighted intersection turn right (Blumaustrasse). Drive beneath the train tracks again, follow the road right around and make the second right into Traunstrasse. At the other end of this residential street, beyond the whitewashed wall, is Villa Trapp (right) nestling in the trees.

Continued from St. Sebastian's church cemetery, page 32:

Mozart, Constanze Weber (b. Jan. 6, 1763 —

d. March 6, 1842). Here lies the wife of the great Wolfgang Amadeus. Mozart met his wife through the opera singer Aloysia Weber, Constanze's sister, whom he was dating at the time! Wolfgang's father, Leopold Mozart, loathed Constanze. In a letter to his father, Wolfgang affectionately described Constanze in a plea to inspire a family-like relationship between the two: *"She is not ugly, but at the same time, far from beautiful. Her beauty consists of two little black eyes and a nice figure. She isn't witty, but has enough common sense to make her a good wife and mother.... She understands house-keeping and has the kindest heart in the world. I love her and she loves me...."* The plea fell on deaf ears and the two parties never reconciled their differences. After Wolfgang's death, Constanze met and eventually married Nikolaus von Nissen, a Danish diplomat. Ironically, Constanze is buried next to Leopold Mozart in Salzburg. Not only does the placement of these two bitter adversaries side by side drive one's curiosity, but Leopold must be turning in his grave since Constanze's headstone (pictured in the middle) hugely dwarfs his (on the right).

Mozart, Leopold (b. Nov. 14, 1719 — d. May 28, 1787). Respected composer, violin teacher, and father of the eminent Wolfgang Amadeus. Leopold was born in Augsburg, Germany, to middle-class parents, Johann Georg Mozart, a bookbinder, and Anna Maria, a homemaker. Leopold left Augsburg at the age of 17 to attend college in Salzburg. It is here that he lived for the rest of his life, becoming a court composer and deputy Kapellmeister for the prince archbishop. Having a secure job, Leopold married his true love, Anna Maria Pertl, in 1747. She gave birth seven times while living in their modest third-floor apartment at Getreidegasse 9—only two survived infancy: Maria Anna (Nannerl) and Wolfgang Amadeus. While Nannerl showed signs of a promising career as a musician, Wolfgang left no doubt that he was a musical genius. Leopold was so proud of his son that he sacrificed his own career as a composer to coach young Amadeus. But as Wolfgang grew older, his desire for individuality and independence put him at odds with his domineering father. Alas, father and son grew apart after the passing of Mozart's mother (in Paris in 1778) and his marriage to Constanze Weber. During this traumatic period, Leopold knew he needed his son more than ever. Fortunately, in 1785, he was able to travel to Vienna, where Wolfgang had moved, to see him one last time. Leopold is buried in St. Sebastian's church cemetery, Salzburg—next to Constanze Weber (see previous entry).

Continued from Mozartplatz, page 12:
Mozart, Wolfgang Amadeus (b. Jan. 27, 1756 — d. Dec. 5, 1791). Regarded as one of the greatest composers of all time, Mozart worked in all musical genres of his era, producing an extraordinary amount of compositions considering his short life. By the time Mozart died at age 35, he had composed 27 piano concertos, 23 string quartets, 17 piano sonatas, more than 50 symphonies, and six major operas, notably "The Marriage of Figaro" (1786), "Don Giovanni" (1787), and "The Magic Flute" (1791). What is perhaps most amazing of all is that Mozart died penniless and was unceremoniously tossed into a commoner's grave for a large amount of people. Except for the gravedigger and the priest, no one showed up to his funeral, not even his wife! A monument (pictured) has been erected in St. Marx Cemetery, Vienna, on the approximate spot where he is believed to be buried. St. Marx Cemetery is located in the suburb of St. Marx, 3 km southeast of central Vienna. A visit is worthwhile. Unique is the fact that the cemetery was closed to burials in 1874; therefore the graveyard appears as it did in the 19th century, presenting an age-old setting of sunken headstones, worn markings, and spiders tending to their intricate webs. To find St. Marx Cemetery, refer to my Vienna guide. GPS: N48 11.031 E16 24.200 (coordinates to cemetery gate). Toilets on right after entering through gate. To reach Mozart, climb main gravel path straight and before Jesus follow the "Mozart Grab" sign left. **Note:** Mozart is the figure depicted on Austria's 1€ coin.

Continued from Drivers/Parking, page 8:

Parking Dial: Before hitting the road, make sure you have the nifty parking dial: a small, 24-hour (blue) cardboard disk that is manually rotated and called a Parkscheibe, or often Parkuhr, in Austria. With the dial properly displayed on your dashboard you will be permitted to park for free in designated areas.

There should be a dial in the glove box (or in the side-door pocket) of your rental car. If your car did not come with a dial, and you haven't yet left the rental agency, go back in and ask for one. If it's too late, you can purchase a dial cheaply at a gas station or magazine shop. When applicable, a diagram of the dial will be featured on local parking signs along with a maximum time limit, like 1 Std. (short for Stunde meaning "hour"). Rotate the dial to the time you pulled into the space (Ankunftszeit, or arrival time) and put it on the dashboard. This way the parking inspector can see when you arrived and if you've overstayed your welcome.

Vignette; Drivers: The maximum speed limit on the Austrian autobahn is 130 kilometers per hour (kph), but to drive on this efficient motorway you are required to have

what's called a "Vignette," or toll sticker affixed to the windshield of your vehicle. The Vignette color this year (2015) is azure (or sky blue). If it is not this color, it's not valid! But even if it is the correct color, it still may not be valid. This is because the Vignette is sold in three (time-constrained) categories: 10 days 8.70€, two months 25.30€, and one year 84.40€. You can obtain this little decal at most any gas station approaching the border (and some gas stations within Austria). **Note:** Affix the Vignette to the inside corner of your windshield or behind the rear-view mirror. (Your rental car may already have a toll sticker from the previous renter; you're in luck if it's still valid.) If you happen to get pulled over without a valid Vignette, the fine is around 240€, on the spot! Lastly, the law requires that you have an international driving permit to drive in Austria (which you can typically pick up for around $15 from your local auto club).

Continued from Drivers/Parking, page 8:
The following examples of **traffic signs** can be commonly seen throughout Austria on its extensive network of roadways.

Do not enter

Closed to all vehicles

One-way street

No parking

No parking or stopping

Autobahn

Short term parking

Tow-away zone

Traffic circle ahead

No left turn

Sharp curve ahead

Curves ahead

Crossroad with non-priority road ahead

No passing

Road narrows ahead

Height restricted to 2.9 meters

Intersection ahead

Slippery when wet

Priority road ahead

Priority road

Yield

Uneven road ahead

Dead end

Train Xing with barrier ahead

Train Xing without barrier ahead

Pedestrian zone

School bus zone

Drive slow — residential zone

Pedestrian crossing

Horn use not allowed

THE END

meet the author

Brett Harriman

Brett Harriman grew up in the seaside town of Dana Point, California, and was fortunate enough to have parents who dragged their kids with them everywhere they went, including on overseas vacations. Thus, the travel bug kicked in early.

Brett's writings are inspired by his love of travel, to which he has driven across America, trekked around Australia, and explored Europe extensively. Brett lived in Australia for a decade and in Europe for five years, where he was an official tour guide for the U.S. Armed Forces in Germany. In that role, Brett led more than 10,000 servicemen and women and their families through many historically rich cities, towns, villages and Alpine hamlets.

In 2011, for all his hard work, Brett was selected by the president of Oktoberfest to represent the USA during the world-famous festival in Munich, Germany.

When he is not in Europe sleuthing out the latest travel information or on tour promoting *Harriman Travel Books*, Brett spends his time in Pahrump (55 miles west of Las Vegas), Nevada, where his parents have retired and he finds serene sanctuary to compile and compose his travel book series, tour-packages, and publishing business.

Brett Harriman enjoying Oktoberfest in Munich, Germany, September 2013

Pictured insets are of guests on Harriman's Oktoberfest tour packages with the exception of the Munich mayor (bottom left) tapping the first keg

Complement this book with other "Harriman Travel Books" and resources

Every year our brand recognition increases across the world together with our array
of destination guides and tour programs.

Harriman
TRAVEL BOOKS

independent
inexpensive
intelligent

If you're headed to Germany or Austria, let
us educate you with local knowledge and history so you can make informed
decisions that save time, as well as money, while leading to new adventures
and acquaintances abroad.

To minimize the advent of stale news and maximize the value of your dollar, we strive to set the gold standard when conducting our research.

Our goal at "Harriman Travel Books" is the trip of your dreams. So come
along, your journey begins *now!*

Printed in Great Britain
by Amazon.co.uk, Ltd.,
Marston Gate.